# Cloning

by Tina Kafka

**LUCENT BOOKS**

*An imprint of Thomson Gale, a part of The Thomson Corporation*

Detroit • New York • San Francisco • New Haven, Conn. • Waterville, Maine • London

This book is dedicated to the
people I love who will someday
benefit from this research.

© 2008 Thomson Gale, a part of The Thomson Corporation.

Thomson and Star Logo are trademarks and Gale and Lucent Books are registered trademarks used herein under license.

For more information, contact
Lucent Books
27500 Drake Rd.
Farmington Hills, MI 48331-3535
Or you can visit our Internet site at http://www.gale.com

LIBRARY OF CONGRESS CATALOGING-IN-PUBLICATION DATA

Kafka, Tina, 1950-
  Cloning / by Tina Kafka.
    p. cm. — (Hot topics)
  Includes bibliographical references and index.
  ISBN 978-1-59018-979-5 (hardcover)
  1. Cloning—Juvenile literature. I. Title.
  QH442.2.K28 2008
  660.6'5—dc22

                                                                          2007036320

ISBN-10: 1-59018-979-5

Printed in the United States of America

# CONTENTS

# FOREWORD

Young people today are bombarded with information. Aside from traditional sources such as newspapers, television, and the radio, they are inundated with a nearly continuous stream of data from electronic media. They send and receive e-mails and instant messages, read and write online "blogs," participate in chat rooms and forums, and surf the Web for hours. This trend is likely to continue. As Patricia Senn Breivik, former dean of university libraries at Wayne State University in Detroit, states, "Information overload will only increase in the future. By 2020, for example, the available body of information is expected to double every 73 days! How will these students find the information they need in this coming tidal wave of information?"

Ironically, this overabundance of information can actually impede efforts to understand complex issues. Whether the topic is abortion, the death penalty, gay rights, or obesity, the deluge of fact and opinion that floods the print and electronic media is overwhelming. The news media report the results of polls and studies that contradict one another. Cable news shows, talk radio programs, and newspaper editorials promote narrow viewpoints and omit facts that challenge their own political biases. The World Wide Web is an electronic minefield where legitimate scholars compete with the postings of ordinary citizens who may or may not be well-informed or capable of reasoned argument. At times, strongly worded testimonials and opinion pieces both in print and electronic media are presented as factual accounts.

Conflicting quotes and statistics can confuse even the most diligent researchers. A good example of this is the question of whether or not the death penalty deters crime. For instance, one study found that murders decreased by nearly one-third when the death penalty was reinstated in New York in 1995. Death penalty supporters cite this finding to support their argument that the existence of the death penalty deters criminals from committing murder. However, another study found that states without the death penalty have murder rates below the national average. This study is cited by opponents of capital punishment, who reject the claim that the death penalty deters murder. Students need context and clear, informed discussion if they are to think critically and make informed decisions.

The Hot Topics series is designed to help young people wade through the glut of fact, opinion, and rhetoric so that they can think critically about controversial issues. Only by reading and thinking critically will they be able to formulate a viewpoint that is not simply the parroted views of others. Each volume of the series focuses on today's most pressing social issues and provides a balanced overview of the topic. Carefully crafted narrative, fully documented primary and secondary source quotes, informative sidebars, and study questions all provide excellent starting points for research and discussion. Full-color photographs and charts enhance all volumes in the series. With its many useful features, the Hot Topics series is a valuable resource for young people struggling to understand the pressing issues of the modern era.

# IAN HAD A LITTLE LAMB

As dusk fell on a Scottish barnyard late one July afternoon in 1996, a white wooly lamb named Dolly was born. This event was both ordinary and earth shattering. Dolly may have looked like any other lamb, but she was unique. Dolly was a clone. In fact, Dolly is widely recognized as the first cloned mammal. Her life began in a laboratory at the Roslin Institute in Scotland, where Ian Wilmut had been trying for a long time to create a sheep that was a genetic twin, or clone, of another sheep. He and his team failed 276 times. But on the 277th try, they finally succeeded, and their success—Dolly—was greeted with both celebration and horror.

Word of Dolly's birth traveled quickly around the world. Legal scholars, religious leaders, and politicians as well as some scientists were quick to raise objections to this new technology. They feared then, as many still do, that cloning crosses boundaries that humans are not prepared to overstep. If it is possible to clone a sheep, many fear that cloning humans is only one small step ahead.

Many people would like to limit all cloning research in order to avoid the possibility of human cloning. Others believe that science has its own momentum, and that it is foolish if not impossible to limit progress because of fears about certain results. Cloning may offer solutions to many of the world's most urgent problems such as hunger, extinction of species, and diseases that plague mankind. It does not make sense to outlaw all cloning, many believe, because the prospect of human cloning is objectionable.

While the future of cloning is still undetermined, scientists continue to refine the techniques involved, although each step along the way presents problems that can result in failure. The process used to clone Dolly is called nuclear transfer. It involves replacing the nucleus of an egg cell, which contains only half of an individual's genetic information, with the nucleus of an adult cell. The nucleus of every adult cell in the body contains all of the genetic information within its chromosomes necessary to create an individual. Cloning Dolly required three sheep. The first sheep provided the adult cell. A second sheep provided the egg. And the third provided the uterus that nurtured Dolly until her birth.

First, the nucleus was removed from the egg. Next, scientists inserted the nucleus from the adult cell into the egg. This new egg now contained all of the genetic information from the first

*Dolly the sheep is widely recognized as the first cloned mammal.*

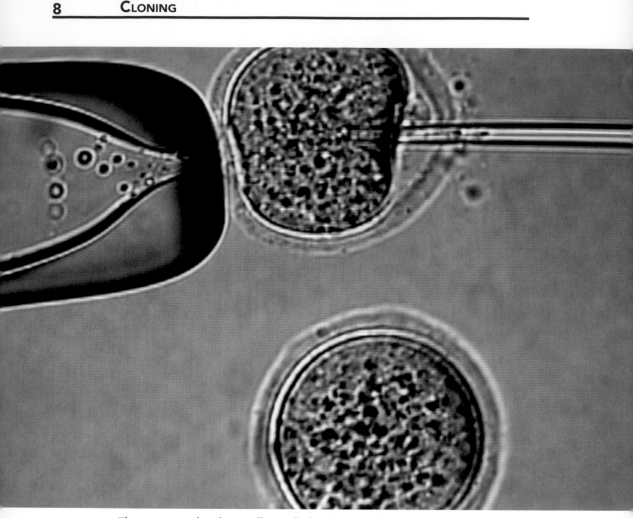

*The process used to clone Dolly is called nuclear transfer, which replaces the nucleus of an egg cell with the nucleus of an adult cell.*

sheep. The new egg was then given a jolt of electricity, and it began to divide in the same way that a normal egg divides after it has been fertilized. Finally, the tiny embryo was implanted in the uterus of the third sheep, where it grew until it was born on that summer day. Dolly's biological mother was the sheep from whom she acquired the nucleus containing her genetic information. Dolly and her mother were identical genetic twins, even though one was a newborn and the other an adult.

Dolly was the result of reproductive cloning, which results in a fully formed organism. Therapeutic cloning, on the other hand, is the term used when the embryo's cells are harvested soon after they begin to divide. These early cells, known as stem cells or master cells, have the potential to become any cell in the body, and, if left alone, develop into a live organism. Within a few days after fertilization, stem cells begin to differentiate, or form into the body's specialized cells. Some become heart cells. Others become nerve cells, or blood cells, or kidney cells. Scientists are now learning how to program stem cells, so they can direct them to become any organ or tissue needed to cure disease and repair tissue damage.

The controversy surrounding therapeutic cloning centers on the destruction of this small cluster of stem cells, called a blastocyst. Scientists, religious leaders, politicians, and the public question whether it is ethical to create, use, or destroy a primitive embryo that has the potential to develop into a living, breathing organism. Although government funding of stem cell research is restricted, privately funded research has progressed quickly in recent years. Scientists are learning how to grow new bone marrow and organs, such as skin, kidneys, and bladders, by creating genetic identical twins, or clones, thereby eliminating organ rejection that results from genetic mismatches.

Cloning may ultimately follow the same course as many other scientific advances that were viewed initially with doubt, debated for many years, and then eventually accepted. The ability of doctors to create a baby by fertilizing an egg in a test tube in 1978, for example, provoked grave concerns at the time. Now it is common for families to rely on various medical interventions to help them create their families. Solutions to some of the most objectionable aspects of cloning are already on the horizon. In fact, certain stem cells have been discovered in other parts of an adult body, which could eliminate the need to create and destroy embryos. Some scientists are developing techniques to reverse the process of cell differentiation; thereby creating new blank cells from mature cells, which can then be reprogrammed as needed.

# CURING DISEASE

While public discussions of cloning quickly turn to fantastic scenarios about creating duplicate movie stars and famous historical figures, most scientists view cloning as a solution to some of the world's most pressing medical problems. Cloning promises to help cure disease, heal devastating injuries, grow organs for transplant, and develop reliable sources for medicines. However, even as scientists in laboratories learn how to clone cells, and create cloned stables of animals with organs that can be transplanted into humans, politicians, religious leaders and the public argue over where to draw the line between what is possible and what is right.

## When Good Cells Go Bad

Many diseases that currently plague people result when cellular systems in the body break down.

Type I diabetes, sometimes called Juvenile Onset Diabetes, for example, is a disease in which the specialized cells in the pancreas, called islet cells, stop secreting insulin. The body needs insulin, which is a hormone, to change sugars, starches, and other foods into energy. Diabetics must closely monitor their insulin levels, and give themselves injections of insulin to make up for their bodies' inability to produce this hormone naturally. Untreated diabetics often suffer devastating consequences such as nerve damage, eyesight problems, and the breakdown of other organs in their bodies. Even diabetics who are careful about monitoring the levels of insulin in their blood often find it difficult to maintain normal levels of insulin.

Douglas Melton, co-director of Harvard's Stem Cell Institute and his colleague, Kevin Eggan, a molecular biologist are targeting diabetes in their stem cell research. Melton has a personal interest in understanding how and why islet cells stop produc-

# Paying a Price for Progress

In his book *The Geneticist Who Played Hoops with My DNA,* David Ewing Duncan reminds readers that potential misuse always accompanies scientific progress. "Lest we forget, periods of explosive scientific achievement and technological breakthroughs have always created the potential for both miracles and horrors. DDT rid the West of malaria-bearing mosquitoes and other pests but poisoned birds and other animals, including humans; electricity lights our cities and powers our factories, but touch a live wire, and zap!; fossil fuels have provided us with fuel to zip about in the air, and on the land and sea, but befoul skies and cause global warming. The list goes on in the pluses and minuses of television that educates and enervates, drugs that cure and cause side effects, cars and airplanes that convey us to places but also turn lethal if they crash and burn."

(Source: David Ewing Duncan, The Geneticist Who Played Hoops with my DNA. New York: HarperCollins, 2005, pg. 9)

ing insulin, since his own two children are diabetics. Before scientists can find a cure for diseases such as diabetes, in which cells stop functioning, however, they need to understand exactly what goes wrong. One way to do that is to use the nuclei from the cells of adult donors with certain diseases to develop embryonic stem cells. Scientists then chemically induce those stem cells to become the type of cells affected by the donor's disease. Since the cells are genetically programmed to stop working properly at some point, scientists can study how their development differs from that of normal cells.

Diabetes is only one of the diseases involving cells with abnormal function that scientists believe may be targeted with embryonic stem cell research. Cloning might also offer the perfect solution for blood diseases such as leukemia, in which the bone marrow stops producing the white blood cells necessary to fight infections. As it is now, a diagnosis of leukemia is often the be-

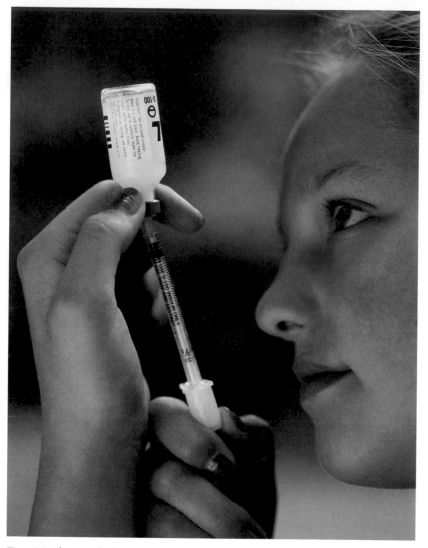

*Type I Diabetes, which requires diabetics to inject themselves daily with insulin, is only one of many diseases that scientists feel stem cell research would benefit.*

ginning of a frantic search for a bone marrow "match," which requires finding a donor—often a relative—who has healthy bone marrow that is genetically compatible with that of the leukemia patient. Bone marrow is then removed from the donor and transplanted into the patient with the hope that the recipient's body will accept the foreign tissue and resume producing healthy white blood cells. However, the chance of a good genetic match is slim, even in the best of circumstances.

Gina Kolata, a science writer for the *New York Times* explains how cloning would improve the prospects of curing leukemia: "But, suppose instead, that scientists could take one of your cells—any cell—and merge it with a human egg. The egg would start to divide, to develop, but it would not be permitted to divide more than a few times. Instead, technicians would bathe it in proteins that direct primitive cells, embryo cells, to become marrow cells. What started out to be a clone of you could grow into a batch of your marrow—the perfect match."[1] Indeed, some believe that this potential cure for leukemia might be less morally troublesome than conceiving a child, as some couples do, in the hopes that it could become a blood marrow donor for an ailing relative.

Diabetes and leukemia are only two of the many diseases targeted by this research. Scientists and the medical community foresee possible stem cell treatments for diseases and injuries of

*A normal brain, on the left, is compared to a brain with Alzheimer's disease. Many in the medical community believe that stem cell research might make it possible to reverse the process of brain degeneration.*

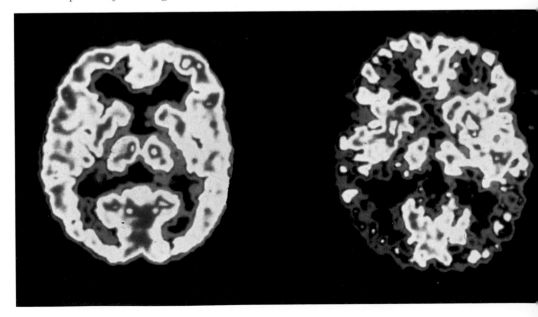

many types when they are able to replace damaged cells from spinal cord injuries, strokes, burns, heart disease, joint diseases, muscular dystrophies and liver diseases. Highly specialized brain cells that regulate the nervous system stop functioning normally in people suffering from Parkinson's and Alzheimer's diseases. If scientists were able to cultivate a steady supply of normal brain cells to replace the cells in the brains of people afflicted with these diseases, it might be possible to reverse the process of brain degeneration.

Cystic Fibrosis (CF) is another disease targeted by cloning research. Some scientists are studying this disease by inserting the human gene that causes CF into sheep cells. These sheep are then bred together. Since both the mother and father have the gene for CF all their lambs will be born with this lung disorder that inhibits normal breathing. These sheep can then be cloned to create many sheep with human cystic fibrosis. While mice with that particular genetic disorder have provided some useful information in the treatment of CF, the lungs of sheep are more similar to those of humans. Moreover, they live longer, which would provide scientists with the ability to study the long-term effects of various treatments for this disease.

However, Mike May, writing in *Scientific American* explains the shadow that lurks in the background of all these potential cures: "Over this incredibly promising work looms a controversy that threatens some stem cell research. It all revolves around one word: embryo."[2] Stem cell treatments inspire debate because, so far, embryos are the only reliable source of stem cells. Whether those embryos are cloned from adult cells or left over from fertility labs, the idea that they have the potential to become fully formed, living, breathing organisms is a concept that many, including religious leaders, politicians, and the public find impossible to reconcile with their moral belief in the sanctity of life.

## Creating Herds of "Pharm" Animals

Cloning cells either to study a disease process or to transplant organs into someone who is suffering from disease or injury is

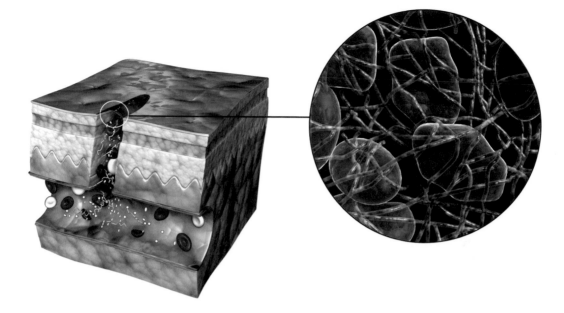

*This damaged blood vessel shows the formation of a blood clot. Hemophiliacs cannot form blood clots and are at serious risk for life-threatening blood loss.*

not the only medical application of this technology. One year after the birth of Dolly, Ian Wilmut cloned another sheep named Polly, whose milk promised to save the lives of human hemophiliacs. Hemophilia is a condition in which the blood cannot form clots, so even minor injuries become life threatening.

Polly began her life like Dolly, by merging the nucleus of a cell from an adult sheep with an egg that had been emptied of its own genetic material. However, in Polly's case, the scientists went even further by adding a human gene to the sheep's cell nucleus. This gene is responsible for making the protein that causes blood to clot. Polly became a so-called "transgenic" sheep, since her genetic makeup now included a human gene. When she matured, her milk contained this human protein. By drinking Polly's milk, human hemophiliacs could then form blood clots. The potential for cloning herds of genetically modified sheep represents the hope for normal lives for hemophiliacs as well as a potential gold mine for the pharmaceutical industry.

While a human gene was added to the transgenic sheep, genes that cause mad cow disease were removed from cow cells before they were cloned. Mad cow disease, also known as *bovine spongiform encephalopathy,* is a crippling degenerative disease of the central nervous system caused by a protein called "prion" that exists in cattle. This disease can be transmitted to humans who either eat infected beef or unknowingly ingest the protein by using medicines made from beef by-products. Hermatech, a biomedical company based in South Dakota removed the gene responsible for prion from cattle skin cells. They then cloned those cells to create 12 genetically altered calves that lacked prion. Though some researchers are concerned that prion may have a purpose that is currently unknown, as of early 2007, the two-year-old calves remain apparently healthy.

However, not everyone agrees that the justification for cloning should be gauged merely by its effects on humans. Dr. Michael W. Fox, a veterinarian who spearheads the movement for the ethical treatment of animals believes that tampering with the genes of animals to create what he calls "manimals," causes the animals to suffer needlessly. Responding to worldwide interest in Dolly at the Roslin Institute, Fox pointed out: "The specter of

## Custom Organs

The Ayala family of California was highly criticized in 1990 when they conceived a baby in the hopes that the baby's blood type would match that of their 16-year-old daughter Anissa, who had leukemia. Baby Marissa was a genetic match to her sister, and when she was six months old, her bone marrow was transplanted into her sister, which saved her sister's life. Then as now, ethicists and the public voice concern about creating either an embryo or a child for the sole purpose of treating someone else's disease.

cloned animal suffering is very real. Dolly-like clones at the Roslin Institute that died soon after birth were larger than normal, putting their mothers at risk, and had congenital abnormalities in their kidneys and cardiovascular systems."[3] In fact, Dolly died at age six of progressive lung disease, usually associated with sheep twice her age. Many scientists suspect that although she looked like a newborn lamb when she was born, she may have inherited the genetic age of her adult mother. Sheep normally live about twelve years.

## Custom Organs

Dolly's cloning in the late 1990s was followed by both exuberant and dire predictions about future applications of clon-

*Robert Lanza has been on the forefront of learning how to use cloning to repair medical problems afflicting humans.*

ing new organs. Proponents predicted that in the near future, it would be possible to grow entire solid organs such as kidneys, livers, and skin by cloning a person's own stem cells and programming them to become the needed tissue. Mike May, writing in *Scientific American* outlines this possibility: "It might even be possible to take a stem cell, nudge it chemically toward making the kind of tissue desired and then control its environment in a way that causes it to build an entire organ. The organ could then be used in someone who needs a transplant, the pinnacle of so-called tissue engineering."[4] If the nucleus from someone's own cell were used to make the stem cell, the body would automatically accept the newly constructed organ since it would be a perfect genetic match.

The race was on to learn how to use cloning to repair some of the worst medical problems afflicting humans. In 2002, Robert Lanza from Advanced Cell Technologies in Worcester, Massachusetts, reported that researchers from his lab had transplanted into cows miniature kidneys created by cloning. Using the same procedure that had been used to clone Dolly, the scientists took the nuclei from the skin cells of one Holstein cow, inserted them into the emptied egg cells of another Holstein, and then implanted the embryos in a third Holstein. Before the calves were quite ready to be born, however, the team of re-

*Dr. David Sachs has worked for twenty years to develop a breed of miniature pigs for a process called xenotransplantation.*

searchers harvested various tissues from the fetuses including heart, muscle, and kidney cells. They then created several miniature kidneys by growing the kidney cells on a specially designed structure resembling a sponge. When the tiny kidneys reached a couple of inches in length, the scientists transplanted them back into the same Holstein whose genes had been cloned originally. Within a few weeks, the small kidneys began producing urine and removing toxins from the Holstein's blood, fulfilling the same function as natural kidneys. This success was hailed as a breakthrough for medical technology as scientists moved closer to realizing their hope of building new organs from an individual's own stem cells, thereby eliminating the problems of organ rejection.

Lanza's enthusiasm for this medical advance was not universal, however. Dr. John Gearhart, a stem cell researcher at Johns Hopkins University expressed concern that harvesting kidney tissue from cow fetuses would alarm the public. An article in the *New York Times* quoted Gearhart: "The experiment's use of cow fetuses will play into fears that scientists are trying to grow clones for direct harvesting of body parts."[5] Lanza's team also transplanted the heart and muscle cells at the same time they transplanted the small kidneys. These cells were never intended to grow into organs, but they were also accepted by the cow's immune system.

## New Human Organs from Cloned Pigs

Cloning technology can also create organs for humans without using human embryos at all. The process is called xenotransplantation—*xeno* means foreign—and involves transplanting cells, tissues, and organs from one species into another. Normal pig organs are too large for humans, but Dr. David Sachs, director of the Transplant Biology Research Center at Massachusetts General Hospital in Boston has worked 20 years to develop a breed of miniature pigs for this purpose. Researchers from Immerge Biotherapeutics, a medical research center inject human genes into the genes of these miniature pigs to make them more compatible with the human immune system. Using the same

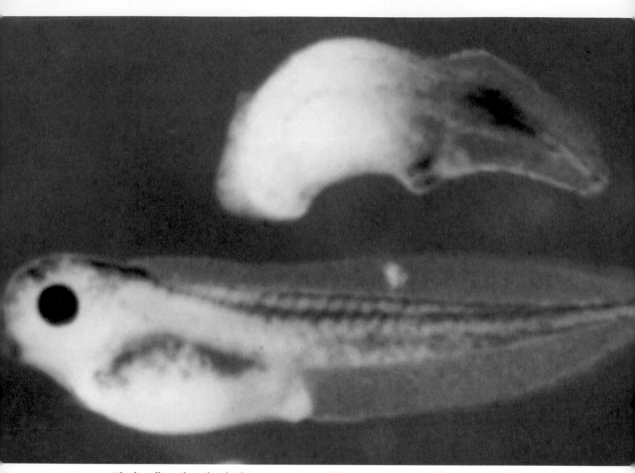

*The headless cloned tadpole, top, was created by scientists to see if the species could be genetically engineered to grow organs, but not a head.*

procedure used by scientists in Scotland to clone Polly, they then transfer the altered genetic material to an egg cell.

The final step, however, is new. Once the embryo reaches the blastocyst stage, researchers remove the genes responsible for creating the protein that a human immune system recognizes as foreign from each resulting embryo. When these baby piglets mature, they are bred with each other. Their offspring are called "double knock-outs," since they are missing both copies of this gene. As a result, their organs will not be rejected by humans, since the human immune system does not recognize them as foreign. There are still many unknowns in this procedure. One potential hurdle is the possible spread of diseases between species, a likely result when immune systems are genetically compatible.

## Headless Clones

As the technology of cloning organs from an individual's own cells slowly advances, an alternate method of growing organs also shows promise. In March 1995 newborn, headless mice were pictured on the cover of *Nature,* a well-known science journal. At first, this appeared to be merely a genetic accident, and the public, though fascinated with the abnormality, was not unduly alarmed. Scientists, however, took note of the fact that Richard Behringer, at the Anderson Cancer Center in Houston, Texas had managed to remove the gene in the mice that is responsible for head development. The mice were perfectly formed except for their missing heads and died as soon as their umbilical cords were severed. Moreover, a mere three years later, the same year that Dolly made her debut, a biologist in England performed a similar experiment, which resulted in the birth of headless frogs.

### HEADLESS BODIES NOT WELCOME

"I doubt that any open society anywhere will accept the laboratory creations of headless but otherwise whole functioning human bodies, even if such creations became feasible. The sense of repugnance is too great, too instinctive, too deep-seated, and too close to being universally held."

—Lee M. Silver, Princeton ethicist

Lee Silver, *Challenging Nature.* New York: HarperCollins, 2006, pg. 171

By this time, the press was more attuned to the presence of cloned animals and quickly publicized the birth of the headless frogs. If headless frogs were possible, were headless humans next, they queried? Journalists, including Charles Krauthammer, joined others in suggesting that people with a failing heart, or diseased kidneys and livers could clone their skin cells and grow new organs without duplicating the essential feature that makes a person undoubtedly human—the head. However, Lee M. Silver, a molecular biologist at Princeton University, who often speaks about ethical issues in science, believes although this may be possible, it is highly unlikely that medical science would approve of this type of gene manipulation. He explains in his book *Challenging Nature*:

> In fact, the development of a human body without a head is not just a hypothetical possibility. In a case reported

*Researchers at the Harvard Stem Cell Institute receive much of their funding from private individuals and foundations.*

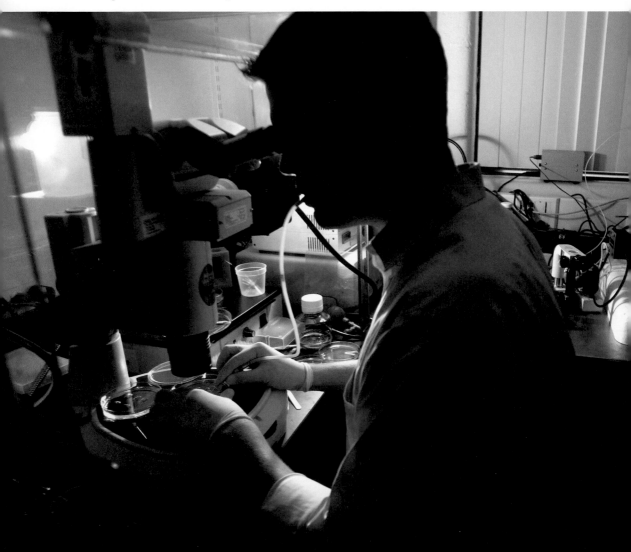

in the American Journal of Obstetrics and Gynecology in 1946, a seven-and-a-half-month-old headless fetus was born completely normal below the neck. With modern medical technology, it would be possible to keep such a body "alive" and growing. Nevertheless, I doubt that any open society anywhere will accept the laboratory creation of headless but otherwise whole functioning human bodies, even if such creations became feasible. The sense of repugnance is too great, too instinctive, too deep-seated, and too close to being universally held.[6]

Silver, like many other scientists, believes that science will develop more acceptable means of reproducing and repairing failing human organs.

## Funding Cloning Research

While these issues are hotly debated, public funding for embryonic stem cell research remains limited, especially in the United States. In August 2001, President George W. Bush cut off federal funding for developing new embryonic stem cell lines. A stem cell line is a population of cells, harvested originally from an embryo that is about five days old, that is grown outside the body in a laboratory. Scientists are able to maintain stem cells in their pre-differentiated state, so they continue to reproduce themselves and retain the potential to become any specialized cell in the body. Before President Bush signed the order restricting new stem cell lines, there were about 22 useable human stem cell lines in the United States. Scientists are concerned, however, that as they age, the cells from these sources have begun to mutate and become contaminated, which makes them unfit for testing new drug therapies.

Moreover, the restriction on federal funding for this research extends beyond the salaries of the scientists. They are forbidden even to use a microscope or any other tool in their research that has been purchased for a lab with federal funds. Bush's order reflects the opinions of many that embryos are a form of life, and that it is immoral to destroy them for any reason. The American Society for the Defense of Tradition, Family, and Property, a conservative group, issued a strong statement that reflects the opinions of many who oppose any human application of this new technology. It says in part: "All human cloning is morally wrong. It can never be purely 'therapeutic.' Cloning—even when euphemistically labeled 'therapeutic' or 'research' cloning—is always reproductive since it always generates a developing human being."[7]

## IMPROVING ORGAN ACCEPTANCE

"The ability to generate immunologically compatible tissue using cloning would overcome one of the major scientific challenges in transplantation medicine, namely, the problem of organ and tissue rejection."
—Robert Lanza, researcher, Advanced Cell Technologies.

John Travis, "Transplant Triumph," Science News Online, June 8, 2002. http://www.sciencenews.org/articles/20020608/fob4.asp

However, restrictions on government funding in the United States have not stopped this research altogether. At the Harvard Stem Cell Institute (HSCI), as at many scientific institutions in the country, much of the funding for this research comes from private individuals and foundations. Howard Heffron, a member of the Harvard Law School Class of 1951, for example donated $5 million to the Harvard Stem Cell Institute. Like Melton, the HSCI's co-director, Heffron's daughter has diabetes and his close friend, the late Law School Dean James Vorenberg suffered from Parkinson's disease. Heffron explains the reason he felt compelled to help fill the funding void left by the federal government: "Knowing these people so intimately, I watched them suffer and deal with the ravages that these diseases bring. I watched helplessly. The potential there [for stem cell research] is so great for helping people in this situation. Here's something to latch onto, to feel like I'm doing something, however indirectly, for these people."[8] Currently, private funds remain the primary source of support for this research in the United States.

## Raising Ethical Issues

The issues raised by cloning research is only a recent example of what happens when new scientific discoveries raise moral and ethical questions that no one yet knows how to answer. An editorial in the New York Times cites examples throughout history: "In the 11th century, European church leaders warned monks that treating illness with medicine showed such a lack of faith in God that it violated holy orders."[9] The editorial written by Deborah Blum, a science writer also tells how religious leaders were outraged when Edward Jenner, an English doctor, discovered a vaccination for smallpox in the 18th century. They preached that a vaccination was overriding God's power to decide matters of life and death. They accused people of being hypocrites if they received a vaccination but still prayed to God.

Cloning raises difficult questions: when does life begin? Should one life be sacrificed to save another? Is it ethical to sacrifice the lives of animals for the health of humans? These issues have yet to be resolved, but as the public wrestles with the moral, ethical, and political implications, the science of cloning moves steadily forward.

# CHAPTER 2

# IMPROVING FOOD

It takes a long time to breed a good cow, or develop an ear of corn that will not succumb to disease or pests. Until recently, breeding was a hit-or-miss enterprise. A farmer takes a good cow and a good bull and hopes for a good calf. Sometimes it works, and sometimes it does not. Cloning could speed up the process and eliminate the element of chance altogether. Cloning offers possibilities for better beef, leaner pork, cows that produce more milk, and eggs with lower cholesterol. Cloning advocates also promote the technology as a way to help provide food to parts of the world where people are starving. However, not everyone is enthusiastic about cloned food.

## Farmers Gamble on Clones

One Montana farmer, Larry Coleman, paid $60,000 to clone his best bull a year after Dolly was born in Scotland. Three baby bulls resulted: First Down, Second Down, and Third Down. Coleman was not alone. Since animal cloning itself was not illegal, many farmers and ranchers cloned their prized livestock, gambling that cloning animals for food would be a new and lucrative direction for the food business. Their risks were expensive. Many farmers paid thousands of dollars to clone their highest-producing dairy cows and prized bulls. Coleman and other farmers had to feed, shelter, and care for the animals longer than expected when a voluntary restriction on the sales of milk or meat from clones went into place in 2001, dashing the farmers' hopes for quick profits.

The restriction also limited the number of clones. In fact, in early 2007, industry officials estimated that only about 500 to 600 cow clones and 200 pig clones occupied the barnyards of this country. An article in the *New York Times* explains why clones will most likely escape the slaughterhouse for now: "Ex-

# Biotechnology Boondoggle?

If scientists at the International Center for the Improvement of Maize and Wheat, known by its Spanish acronym Cimmyt (pronounced SIM-it) can find a way to develop self-cloning corn, poor farmers should reap the rewards. Many plants, including dandelions, wheat, and rice clone themselves naturally. The process is called apomixes. However, according to an article in the *Wall Street Journal*, many critics do not trust Cimmyt's biotechnology program to serve poor farmers. Reporter Daniel Charles explains: "One encounters antipathy toward biotechnology, in fact, within Cimmyt as well. Cimmyt's crusty plant breeders sometimes dismiss their organization's biotech program as a boondoggle, an expensive fad that has squandered millions of dollars without delivering, so far, a single useful product to farmers. Many resent the deals—accompanied by confidentiality clauses and agreements to protect intellectual property—Cimmyt's biotechnologists have struck with companies. The center should be accountable only to the world's poorest farmers, these critics say, not multinational biotechnology empires."

Daniel Charles, "Corn that Clones Itself Could Help Feed the Poor," *Wall Street Journal*, February 28, 2003. http://www.agbios.com/static/NEWSID_4087.php

perts say that cloning is too expensive to be used to make animals only to grind them into hamburger or even to milk them. Rather farmers and breeders are cloning prized livestock so they can then be used for breeding using more conventional means of reproduction."[10] The food industry predicts that cloning will allow the development of beef and pork with lower fat content. Some hope to genetically engineer animals to be resistant to various diseases before they are cloned.

## FDA Rules on Cloned Food

Everything changed for the cloned food business at the beginning of January 2007. That is when the United States Food and Drug Administration (USFDA) ruled that meat, milk, and eggs

*A rancher stands with his five cloned bulls. Many farmers and ranchers clone their livestock hoping that cloning animals for food will be a lucrative business in the future.*

from cloned animals are as safe to eat as ordinary meat, milk, and eggs. That long awaited decision was a relief to ranchers and farmers across the United States, where clones grazed, rooted in pig sties, and nested unaware that their fate rested with the FDA's decision.

As some applaud and others condemn cloned food's official entry into the marketplace, many concede that cloned food has sneaked into the butcher shop already. Since cloned animals were not yet approved, but trial cloning was well underway awaiting the FDA's decision, baby animal clones had been distributed to young members of farm clubs around the country— known as the club calf circuit, although it also includes swine, goats, and chickens. These youngsters raise their clones and then bring them to county fairs and farm competitions across the United States. At the end of the competitions, the animals are sold to the highest bidder and slaughtered for food. In addition, many farmers use their clones as regular breeding stock and the FDA has no way to keep track of their offspring.

## CLONEBURGER SPECIAL

"Cloning technology will offer yet another tool to enable biologists and animal breeders to make foods more consistent, nutritious, and tasty. The controversy over cloning is less about the possible risks of a "cloneburger" than about the bad-faith attempts by activists to delay or derail a promising technology."

Henry I. Miller, "These Products are Long Overdue," *San Diego Union Tribune*, January 3, 2007, pg. B7

Many biotech companies did not wait for the FDA's approval to develop cloning technology. They assumed that the FDA would eventually give cloned food its stamp of approval. The United States Institute of Science and Technology, for example, provided millions of dollars in research grants to biotech companies to fund research into the technology necessary to clone chickens on a massive scale. They anticipated the possibility of producing billions of clones from genetically engineered chickens whose eggs might be low in cholesterol or free from the salmonella bacteria that causes food poisoning. These companies anticipated that once the FDA gave its official approval they could grow billions of chicken clones each year that would lay identical eggs or provide identical breasts, drumsticks, and other edible body parts for American chicken dinners.

## The 'Yuck Factor'

Although the FDA approved of food from cloned animals, overcoming public distaste for cloned food may be the biggest obstacle facing the future fortunes of farmers who clone. While science writers and consumer reporters delight in poking fun at "clonedogs" and "cloneburgers," opposition to eating food from clones is no laughing matter.

Polls conducted by various consumer groups agree that the majority of the American public is squeamish about eating food from clones. This resistance, often referred to as the 'yuck factor,' is widespread. According to a survey in 2004 by the International Food Information Council, 62 percent of consumers said they would be very unlikely to buy meat, milk, and eggs from cloned animals. Another poll conducted by the well-known polling company Gallup also found that 64 percent of American consumers believe that cloning animals is immoral. An article in the *Washington Post* describes consumer reaction to eating food from clones, sometimes referred to as "Frankenfoods," (a reference to Dr. Frankenstein's monster): "Consumer groups counter that many Americans are likely to be revolted by the idea of serving clone milk to their children or tossing meat from the offspring of clones onto the backyard grill. This "yuck factor" has come to light repeatedly in public opinion surveys."[11]

Some people were able to sample cloned food even before FDA approval. Workers at one biotechnology company had the opportunity to conduct taste-tests of cloned ingredients while awaiting the FDA decision. They found that food from clones was just as appetizing as food prepared from ingredients that were not cloned. An article in the *San Diego Union Tribune* tells of the culinary adventures of these employees: "Months before the FDA's announcement that meat from cloned animals is safe to

*This poster from the Center for Food Safety shows the concern over the introduction of cloned foods into the marketplace.*

eat, employees at Cyagra were carving into cloned steaks several times a week. When those ran out, they ate cloned hamburgers, tacos, lasagna, and meat loaf."[12] They compared samples from eleven clones and eleven ordinary cattle. Their conclusion: they tasted exactly the same.

Scientists are concerned about more than just taste, however. Moreover, the safety of food is an international concern, since meat is an important export. Japanese scientists from the Operation of Urgent Research for Utilization of Clone Technology, a biotech company in Japan conducted extensive studies of

*Demonstrators wearing cow costumes march to voice their revulsion toward certain cloned foods in the marketplace.*

cloned meat in 2004. They analyzed its chemical structure and studied its reactions to simulated human digestive systems. They then fed the meat from cloned cattle to rats for 14 weeks and subjected the rats to tests of their motor activity, strength, and reflexes. Finally they killed the rats and conducted autopsies to determine whether the clone-fed rats differed in any way from rats fed regular meat. They found no biological differences.

## Science vs. Emotion

Ranchers and farmers who had been forced to withhold their cloned products from the market and biotech companies hoping to capitalize on cloning technology were not the only ones who hailed the FDA decision. Many scientists see cloning as an important way to produce higher quality, healthy foods. They believe that cloning promises the possibility of better quality products such as beef and pork with less fat and more protein.

Eventually these products will be available to all consumers. The Federation of Animal Science Societies drafted a statement endorsing the FDA's approval of cloned food that was signed by 246 prominent scientists around the world, including Ian Wilmut, Dolly's breeder. The Federation even placed an ad in a daily paper that pictured a cloned cow grazing with her calf. "What's wrong with this picture?" the ad asked, "Absolutely nothing."[13] Dairy farmers hope to clone their best milk producers. The average cow produces about 15,000 gallons of milk each year, while some super producers make as much as 40,000 gallons of milk. The possibility of creating entire herds of super milk producers is enticing to dairy farmers. The FDA considers only scientific information in its decisions about cloned food.

However, while public opinion does not influence the FDA, its decisions do not necessarily change public opinion either. Despite the FDA's ruling, many people still do not trust the safety of cloned foods. David Schubert a researcher at the Salk Institute in La Jolla, California has concerns. He points to the high levels of hormones used to trick an animal's body into becoming pregnant with another animal's clone. He claims those hormones will inevitably enter the food supply along with the animals' body parts. Furthermore, Schubert points out that many clones are born with defective immune systems and need extensive treatment with antibiotics to treat or prevent infections.

He compares the current controversy over cloning to the toxic consequences of pesticides, herbicides and fertilizers, which were approved before knowledge of their deadly consequences was fully known. In an editorial in the *San Diego Union Tribune,* Schubert writes: "The reason the U.S. population does not spend much time thinking about the origin of its food is because it believes the FDA is doing the necessary safety testing. In fact, there is not required safety testing for genetically modified crops; there will be none for cloned animals."[14] Schubert accuses the FDA of serving the interests of biotech companies and large agricultural businesses over public safety.

## Self-Basting Cows

Although the FDA ruled in early 2007 that cloned animal products are safe to eat, many consumers express concern. They point to widespread use of chemicals in agriculture that were once deemed safe, but are now known to cause cancer, birth defects, and environmental problems. Genetically modified (GM) foods once promised to make food cheaper and eliminate world hunger. Only later has the public discovered that GM foods sometimes cause food allergies and other nutritional problems. In addition, ten years after GM foods entered the marketplace, food prices are higher, and world hunger persists. David Schubert, a professor at the Salk Institute for Biological Studies in La Jolla, California, points out how genetic solutions sometimes lead to new problems. "Since the super milk producer gets infections of her udder, the high-tech solution was to make a transgenic cow that produces its own antibiotics. Next up, cattle that make their own barbecue sauce."

David Schubert, "Food from Cloned Animals," *San Diego Union Tribune,* January 3, 2007, pg. B7.

*Dr. Ian Wilmut, who created Dolly the sheep in 1997, signed a statement along with other scientists endorsing the FDA's approval of cloned food.*

Food safety is not the only concern. Various animal rights groups also express opposition to cloning animals for the benefit of humans. Dr. Michael W. Fox, a veterinarian who leads the movement for the ethical treatment of animals believes that animal cruelty is an inevitable outcome of animal cloning. He explains in his book *Beyond Evolution:* "The specter of cloned animal suffering is very real. On a British Broadcasting Company (BBC) TV documentary entitled 'Hello Dolly,' the founders of Granada Genetics in Texas, the first company to market cloned cattle, admitted that their venture failed because many cow clones were abnormally large, had enlarged hearts, and developed diabetes."[15] Many clones die during gestation or shortly after birth. Others are born with deformed heads or limbs, or abnormal lungs, hearts, and other organs. Scientists still do not know why Dolly the sheep developed lung disease and arthritis and died prematurely. Many scientists believe that all animal clones have subtle genetic defects, and that further study is needed before humans consume them. Fox and many others believe that it is morally wrong to exploit animals in this way.

## Read the Label

The 2007 decision by the FDA that cloned food did not differ from regular food set off a new firestorm of controversy. Now that cloned foods are deemed safe, arguments rage about whether cloned food should be labeled so that consumers know that they are feeding their families food from clones. The Federal Food, Drug and Cosmetics Act requires that food labels are not misleading. Moreover, federal law prohibits labels that might be misunderstood by consumers, even if they are literally accurate.

Henry I. Miller, a physician at the Hoover Institution who directed the FDA's Office of Biotechnology from 1989-1993 explains when he uses the example of placing a 'cholesterol-free' label on a bunch of broccoli. While the label is, indeed, accurate, since broccoli does not contain cholesterol, consumers could conclude that the labeled broccoli differs from other broccoli in that way. Miller explains how labels on food from clones could also be misinterpreted: "The presence of a label would be misconstrued by some consumers as suggesting that food from cloned animals differs in an important way such as safety or nutrition."[16]

While food industry officials and various consumer groups wrangle over labeling cloned foods, one Congresswoman has introduced a bill to the U.S. Senate that would make it mandatory to label food that comes from cloned animals. Senator Barbara A. Mikulski, a Democratic senator from Maryland, introduced the Cloned Food Labeling Act in early 2007. This bill requires that all food that comes from a cloned animal or the offspring of a cloned animal be clearly labeled. Senator Mikulski reflects the feelings of many Americans who believe they have the right to know the origin of their food: "Consumers won't be able to tell which foods came from a cloned animal. Which burger is really 'Dolly on a bun?' Should Americans be compelled to eat anything a scientist can produce in the laboratory? Just because they can make it, should Americans be required to eat it? Of course not! The public deserves to know if their food comes from a cloned animal."[17] The bill is still before Congress. Organic food labels, however, are already clear. An advisory panel to the United States Department of Agriculture's National Organic Program voted unanimously in Spring 2007 that any food labeled 'organic' is guaranteed to be free of any ingredients from a cloned animal or its offspring.

*Many senators, including Carole Migden from California, are calling for legislation that would require that milk and meat products from cloned animals be clearly labeled.*

## Cloned Corn on the Cob—Who Benefits?

While cloning animals for food represents technology on its cutting edge, cloning plants is as natural as eating. More than 300 species of plants reproduce themselves by natural cloning. Most tree fruits and nuts are natural clones, as are pineapples, potatoes, and onions.

The word "clone" itself is derived from a Greek word that referred to a twig used to propagate plants. In 1903, Herbert J. Webber of the United States Department of Agriculture proposed that an English version of the Greek word—clon—be used to refer to plants that reproduced themselves asexully. *Clon*

*More than 300 species of plants reproduce themselves by natural cloning, or asexual reproduction.*

soon became *clone* to refer to any form of life that reproduced in this way.

In asexual reproduction, everything needed to reproduce is contained within one organism, as opposed to sexual reproduction, which requires a male and a female. Various plants have different ways of cloning themselves. Some, like the potato, reproduce themselves using an underground stem—the tuber that is eaten roasted, baked, and fried. Moreover, some plants, such as cacti and succulents, clone themselves by developing complete new plants from one leaf. While this trait is useful in some ways, it can also be dangerous. The Irish potato famine in the 1840s, which resulted in widespread hunger and disease, was the result of a single fungus that caused a disease called blight. The potatoes—being genetically identical—were unable to resist the fungus, and over one million people died in a three-year period between 1846 and 1849, either from starvation or illnesses made worse by malnutrition.

The dual consequences—positive and negative—of tampering with plant genes is a controversy that has arisen in recent years as scientists have identified the genes that are responsible for certain features of plants and then modified them in various ways. Scientists have learned how to genetically modify plants to contain their own insecticides, for example. Other plants have been genetically engineered to resist certain weed killers, so a field can be sprayed without damaging the food crop. Scientists at the International Center for the Improvement of Maize and Wheat—known as Cimmyt—near Mexico City, are developing a variety of corn that clones itself. Corn, a food staple in much of the world, is a plant that naturally reproduces by dispensing pollen from its tassels, which then fertilizes nearby ears of corn. However, in order to maintain high quality corn seed, farmers must buy new seed each year. This is a hardship for many poor farmers. If scientists at Cimmyt succeed, poor farmers could plant fields of productive, hardy strains of corn, and produce enough corn both to feed the population and plant for the following year's crop. However, this advance is not without its critics. Two strong forces that are normally opposed to each other are both skeptical about the future of cloned corn.

# Natural Cloning in Plants

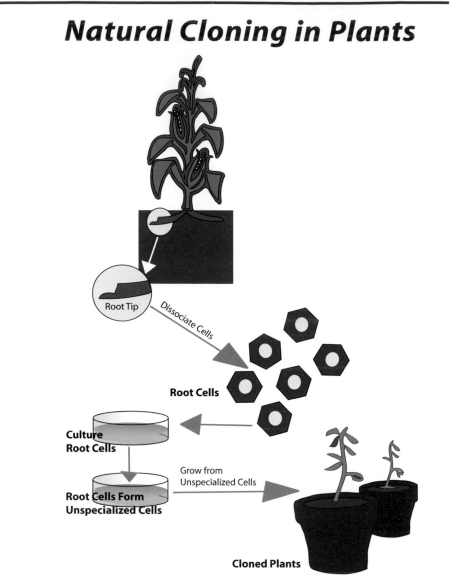

Root Tip

Dissociate Cells

**Root Cells**

**Culture Root Cells**

**Root Cells Form Unspecialized Cells**

Grow from Unspecialized Cells

**Cloned Plants**

*HowStuffWorks, Inc. Available online at: http://science.howstuffworks.com/ cloning1.htm*

## Profits from Cloning Crops

First of all, many scientists and members of the public are opposed in general to genetic engineering. There is a perception among many people that it is wrong to tamper with nature in such an extreme way. And corn is especially revered in Mexico.

An article in the *Wall Street Journal* describes Mexico's relationship to this grain:

> If opponents of genetic engineering have their way, no genetically engineered corn will ever grow in Mexican soil. Mexico is the ancestral homeland of corn, the place where ancient peoples first domesticated this crop. Mexican farmers maintain an astonishing number of corn varieties. Adapted to an enormous array of climates, Mexico's corn comes with kernels in black, white, and every color in between.[18]

Many people also fear that genetically modified corn will displace the traditional varieties grown in hundreds of small fields throughout the country.

Seed companies also oppose the wide distribution of self-cloning corn, since they reap enormous profits from the sale of corn seed to farmers all over the world. Although Cimmyt's research into this corn has corporate sponsors, many skeptics believe that corporate support is ultimately self-serving. The ability to sow corn that clones itself is useful when developing better corn. But if corporations pay for the research and then patent the results, then they also control the use of the self-cloning seeds. Many believe that seed companies are more interested in the ability to turn off the gene responsible for cloning. In this way, they keep self-cloning corn out of the hands of local farmers. The article in the *Wall Street Journal* explains how these tensions affect the field of biotechnology: "Even before the first self-cloning corn seeds are ready to be sown, the prospect looms that political debates and corporate interests will poison the ground. And that would be a blight not only on the future of poor farmers, but also on the reputation of agricultural biotechnology—a field already dogged by accusations that its science has not done enough for the human good."[19] Cimmyt's scientists insist that their corporate sponsors have given them complete freedom to distribute the self-cloning corn to poor farmers in developing nations. Moreover, they see no conflict in accepting financial support from large seed companies.

*Workers prepare graft clones of cacao leaves. Many people are concerned that genetically modified crops will displace traditional varieties.*

Corn is not the only food crop with cloning in its future. The Agricultural Research Service, a branch of the U.S. Department of Agriculture is also working on cloning the genes in soybeans to improve soy's nutritional quality. Soy is commonly used in infant formulas, tofu, yogurt, and the oils used in mayonnaise, cake frosting, and chocolate bars.

The more scientists learn about genetics, the more capable they become of manipulating life itself. Pigs with organs that can be transplanted into people, plants that produce medicine and their own insecticides are accomplishments that are both wondrous and terrifying. However, even as scientists learn how to clone an identical twin of a plant or animal, mysteries remain. The biggest mystery ultimately may be whether these tools will primarily help solve complex global problems such as hunger and disease, or whether they will primarily reap profits for those who fund the research.

# CHAPTER 3

# SAVING THE ANIMALS

Many species of wild animals are disappearing from the earth as environmental changes and human populations threaten their habitats. Approximately 100 species become extinct each day. Cloning could be a way to stem this trend and preserve the biodiversity of the planet. However, some conservationists worry that an emphasis on cloning will overshadow efforts to preserve disappearing habitats. Though it seems far-fetched, there are those who dream of parks where extinct animals roam. Many pet owners hope to clone beloved family pets—even though critics disapprove, since so many homeless pets await adoption. As with other cloning applications, the legal and ethical issues raised by cloning animals reflects society's deep conflicts about interfering with life at its most basic level.

## SAVE PEOPLE OR ANIMALS?

"Should we save endangered species by preserving their habitats even if it costs the lives of a million Africans? Greenpeace opposed introduction of genetically modified crops to preserve the environment in Zimbabwe, even though its people were starving."

Gregory Pence, *After Dolly Who's Still Afraid?* Lanham: Rowman & Littlefield Publishers, Inc., January 2005, pg. 32.

## New Cloning Challenges

Once scientists realized that sheep could be cloned, they began to experiment with cloning other species. The *Washington Post* reported that at a meeting on mammal cloning held in June 1998 in Arlington, Virginia, scientists from labs around the country and Europe reported that cows, sheep, pigs and monkeys were pregnant with clones. Less than a year after Dolly's birth, Charlie and George arrived in Texas—two calves cloned by Steve Stice and James Robl of Advanced Cell Technologies (ACT) in Massachusetts. Cloning specialists celebrated the fast progress of cloning technology. ACT also revealed the imminent birth of a litter of cloned piglets. Another biotechnology company, ABS Global in Wisconsin proudly announced the birth of a healthy baby bull named "Gene."

While these scientists were anticipating how cloning could benefit the treatment of human disease, and farmers were hoping to increase their food production, experts in animal conservation had their eyes on cloning for a different reason. They hoped to clone animals whose populations had dwindled to only a few remaining individuals confined to zoos. However, the limited

# Cloning Progress Since Dolly

In recognition of the ten year anniversary of the birth of Dolly the cloned sheep, the National Public Radio show "All Things Considered," broadcast a series of questions and answers about ways in which the science of cloning animals has advanced since Dolly's birth:

**Q: In the decade since Dolly was revealed to the world, what practical advances in cloning have been made?**

Although cloning still is not an efficient process, scientists have become more efficient at making cloned animals. It still requires dozens, if not hundreds, of fresh eggs to make a cloned embryo, and then only a small fraction of the cloned embryos will produce a live birth after being transferred to an animal's womb. But the process is efficient enough to make it possible to clone prized barnyard animals for breeding stock, and it may be possible to insert genes into these animals that will give them desirable traits. For example, scientists have inserted a gene into pigs that causes them to produce a kind of fat that is healthier for the human diet.

Joe Palca, "Cloning Q&A: What Have We Learned Since Dolly?" All Things Considered, National Public Radio, February 22, 2007. http://www.npr.org/templates/story/story.php?storyid=7555718

*Newborn transgenic cows, George (left) and Charlie, arrived in Texas less than a year after the birth of Dolly the sheep.*

numbers of these endangered animals presented some unique challenges, since even a clone needs a mother.

Scientists know that any pregnancy is risky, even in the best of circumstances, but a pregnancy that results from cloning can be especially difficult. In order to trick her body into accepting the pregnancy, large amounts of hormones are administered to the surrogate mother. Since the animals to be cloned are already endangered, scientists are reluctant to risk the lives of any of the precious few remaining individuals. Also, from a practical standpoint, it is complicated to round up the few remaining females of an endangered species. However, scientists and animal conservationists hoped that if one ewe can bear another sheep's lamb, it may be possible for an animal of one species to give birth to a baby of a different species. These speculations bore fruit in January 2001, when scientists at ACT proudly announced that Bessie the cow had given birth to Noah the gaur, an endangered Asian ox.

## It's a Gaur!

Baby Noah was greeted worldwide with headlines and fanfare, but the celebration was short lived. Two days after the small brownish-black calf with white legs was born and took his first steps, he died of a common infection. ACT scientists claimed Noah's death was unrelated to his unusual beginnings. However, they admitted that even the chances of his birth were slim. To clone Noah, ACT removed the nuclei from 692 cow eggs and fused them with skin cells from one dead gaur. Of those eggs, only 81 developed into blastocysts of 100 cells. Scientists im-

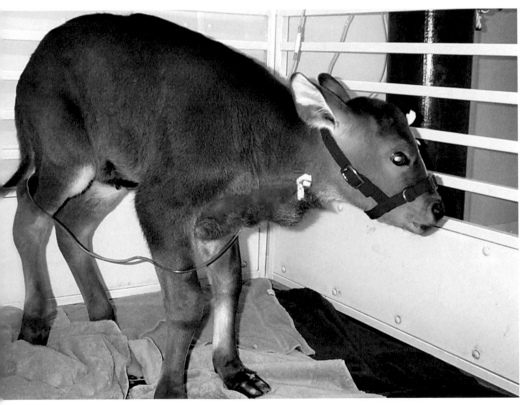

*In January 2001, scientists announced they had successfully cloned a gaur, the first endangered species to be cloned. Scientists believe that many endangered species can be saved from extinction through cloning.*

planted half of those blastocysts into 32 cows. Eight pregnancies resulted. Noah was the sole gaur that developed to full term and was born alive.

Robert Lanza, a lead ACT researcher explains the significance of Noah's short life: "While Noah died from a common bacterial infection, this birth was a new day in the conservation of his kind as well as in the preservation of many other endangered species. Perhaps, most important, he was living, mooing proof that one animal can carry and give birth to the exact genetic duplicate, or clone, of an animal of a different species.[20]

Lanza envisioned an ark filled with cloned endangered species, which explained the name "Noah" for the new clone. He also announced plans to clone a Sumatran tiger. Writing in the widely distributed journal *Scientific American,* Lanza revealed that the work of ACT had resulted in some startling births. Ordinary house cats had given birth to two endangered wild felines: an endangered African wildcat, named "Ditteaux," and an Indian desert cat. A common African antelope called an eland had delivered a rare bongo antelope, and a common white-tailed deer served successfully as surrogate mother to a rare red deer. Lanza also voiced hope that future cloning might rescue the cheetah from extinction, since only 12,000 individuals still roam southern Africa.

## A Frozen Zoo

While scientists at the San Diego Zoo's Center for the Reproduction of Endangered Species (CRES) were not sure exactly why they began collecting live cells from endangered species and freezing them in the 1970s, their foresight and cloning technology began to fuse in ways they never anticipated. Called the "Frozen Zoo," the four deep freeze tanks contain cells of some of the rarest creatures on the earth, including giant pandas, condors, and California grey whales. The Frozen Zoo has a benefit beyond providing intact cells to clone, however.

As the number of individuals of a species dwindles, the gene pool also shrinks. Certain genetic traits that might otherwise disappear are, instead, emphasized as inbreeding occurs between closely related individuals. This often results in unhealthy or deformed animals. By preserving the cells from individual animals that die, scientists can maintain a healthier and more diverse gene pool. In this way, genetic traits that have disappeared from living members of a species can be preserved and reintroduced when scientists create a new clone. According to Dr. Oliver Ryder, director of the Frozen Zoo, "This isn't a stunt. It's a new arena and we have the responsibility to see what benefits may come from this technology."[21]

One of the first species to benefit from the fusion of frozen cells and cloning technology is the endangered banteng, also known as Bali cattle, hunted almost to extinction for its slender, curved horns. Eleven ordinary cows became pregnant with banteng calves in 2002, and though scientists happily anticipated a small herd, only two baby banteng clones were born alive. However, scientists still cel-

*San Diego Zoo geneticist Oliver Rider holds up a refrigerated mammal cell at the Zoo's research lab. Called the "Frozen Zoo," the tanks contain some of the rarest creatures on the globe.*

ebrated the progress represented by the birth of animals that were cloned from one species and borne by another.

While many species of endangered animals could benefit one day, the prospect of cloning the giant panda is one that both tempts and frustrates scientists. Notoriously difficult to breed in captivity—even in the usual manner—the wild panda population has diminished to only about 1,700 individuals that still roam the bamboo forests of southwest China. In 2004, China announced plans to protect its national symbol by creating a panda gene bank containing cells from 21 living pandas and five that had died, including Hsing Hsing and Ling Ling, a famous panda pair that once lived in the National Zoo in Washington, D.C. Eventually China will collect cell samples from the 161 pandas that live in special reserves in that country for eventual cloning.

Chinese scientists have failed repeatedly so far to clone a panda. First of all, it is hard to find a suitable surrogate. So far, panda clones have been implanted in rabbits and cats, since the newborn panda is about the same size as a tiny kitten (or a stick of butter), and rabbits and cats are readily available. However, as scientists learn more about the importance of the surrogate to a clone's development, they now believe that American black bears may provide better surrogate mothers for pandas, since they are more closely related genetically than either rabbits or cats.

## To Clone or Not to Clone

As exciting as it is to envision saving endangered species, cloning them is not universally applauded. Some biologists voice concern that cloning inevitably leads to a population with too much genetic similarity. This could lead to disastrous consequences if every member of an animal population were susceptible to the same diseases. Conservationists question the wisdom of cloning members of a species that no longer exists in the wild. These clones could only survive in zoos, since their natural habitats have disappeared. However, the objection most frequently voiced to the cloning of endangered species is that cloning will overshadow efforts to preserve the biodiversity of the earth.

## A BIG DEAL

"Canon, the company that makes photocopiers, came out with an advertisement featuring two identical sheep. 'Big deal. We've been making perfect copies for years,' the ad said."

Quoted in Kolata, *Clone*, pg. 34

Many environmentalists reject the notion that the number of living species is a valid measure of the wealth of life on earth. They believe that scientists should place higher value on educating people about the complex interdependence of life and engaging them in its preservation. Gregory Pence, who writes frequently about the ethical issues of cloning, addresses the conflicts between environmentalists and the biotech industry,

# How to Make a Dinosaur

In the book *Jurassic Park* (later made into a movie of the same name) author Michael Crichton describes a formula to bring dinosaurs, which have been extinct for 65 million years, back to life. This website devoted to unusual scientific topics details the recipe:

STEP 1) Find a piece of amber with a bloodsucking insect from the dinosaur era trapped in it.

STEP 2) Extract the blood that insect sucked from a dinosaur.

STEP 3) Use the dinosaur's genetic code (DNA) found in the blood cells as blueprints for another dinosaur. If pieces of the DNA are missing, fill in the gaps with frog DNA.

STEP 4) Use these blue prints to create a dinosaur egg.

STEP 5) Hatch the dinosaur in an incubator.

STEP 6) Raise the dinosaur to full size.

STEP 7) Enjoy!

Quoted in The Unmuseum, "How to Make a Dinosaur," http://unmuseum.mus.pa.us/dnadino.htm

which provides much of the funding for cloning research: "This response illustrates a disturbing new alliance against science and technology by environmentalists, animal rights groups and others. None of these groups sees biotechnology as providing useful tools to manage the environment, probably because they do not trust business or government to do so."[22] Oliver Ryder of CRES is one of many scientists who believe that cloning has an important role in species preservation, but that bans on hunting, habitat preservation, and public awareness of the value of biodiversity are ultimately more important.

## Oh Give Me a Home Where the Wooly Mammoths Roam

While many scientists and conservationists focus on stemming the rushing tide of endlessly disappearing species, others have their hopes set on reviving species that are already extinct. The movie *Jurassic Park* directed by Steven Spielberg in 1993 was a work of science fiction, but it tapped into a long-held hope that it might really be possible to revive a dinosaur or two. A Japanese scientist, Akira Iritani, announced plans to do just that.

In 2002, Iritani publicized his plans to create "Pleistocene Park," a preserve for resurrected wooly mammoths, a prehistoric elephant that thrived during the Pleistocene Era. Wooly mammoths, bison, and other jumbo plant-eating creatures roamed the vast Siberian grasslands in Asia until the end of the last ice age, about 11,000 years ago. Iritani's plans include providing refuge for other prehistoric animals as well, including the resurrected wooly rhinocerous—extinct for 10,000 years. Many consider Iritani's plans far-fetched, but a Russian scientist has purchased and enclosed 160-square kilometers in the remote Siberian wilderness to provide grazing lands for the wooly mammoths he hopes Iritani will clone.

Cloning the wooly mammoth is a monumental scientific challenge, however. There are several obstacles. The main challenge is finding a cell with an intact nucleus. While scientists have discovered fossils and even reconstructed entire mammoth skeletons in museums, intact cells have still never been found. Scientists pin their hopes on finding a perfectly preserved fro-

*Japanese scientists are trying to clone prehistoric animals such as the wooly mammoth, which is a monumental scientific challenge.*

zen cell from a mammoth that may have met its end in an icy crevasse. Writing in Cosmos, an online science magazine, writer Jacqui Hayes contrasts the Siberian wastelands to San Diego's Frozen Zoo: "Nature has its own frozen zoo. Unlike the youthful San Diego Zoo, in existence for only 25 years, the vast waste-lands of Siberia have held animals trapped in permafrost for as long as 200,000 years."[23]

In the past, researchers have found pieces of preserved mammoth skin and muscle in Siberia. While most of those cells were no longer intact, they have been able to study parts of those cells and compare them to those of living elephants. As scientists learn more about the sequences of the genes in each organism's strands of DNA, it may one day be possible to synthesize the missing pieces and build an entire set of wooly mammoth chromosomes.

The scientists will also face the challenge of finding a suitable surrogate for a cloned mammoth baby. The more they learn, the more evident it appears that scientists still do not completely understand the biological role of the surrogate. While techni-

# A Warning in a Striped Coat

Scott Weidensaul, a naturalist who writes frequently about animals, their natural habitats, and the environment questions the wisdom of cloning the thylacine, also known as the Tasmanian tiger: "Today the thylacine is both a wraith and a warning, clad in a striped coat. Clone one, the skeptics say, and it becomes a novelty; clone a couple of dozen and they become a conservation headache—a population that needs a home, and management, and oversight, just another endangered species in a world already parceling out limited resources to so many others. It might also deaden the public's worry over critically rare organisms, by planting the comfortable but incorrect notion that there's a scientific quick fix even for something as permanent as extinction."

Scott Weidensaul, "Raising the Dead," *Audubon,* May, 2002. http://www.audubonmagazine.org/features0205/thylacine.html

cally, scientists are becoming adept at replacing one nucleus with another, there are other factors at work too. Scientists are still learning, for example, how other parts of the egg affect the embryo's growth. Hayes frames some of the questions that plague the scientific community: "Are clones with a mother from a different species a true copy? Does it matter? What about the natural bacteria in the gut, passed from mother to offspring? How would a monkey, whose mother was a rabbit or a baboon, fare outside a zoo?"[24] These questions need to be answered before rare, still-to-be-discovered wooly mammoth cells are squandered in experiments with remote chances of success.

## A Bouncing Baby Thylacine?

While the ability to clone the residents for a Pleistocene Park has not yet met with success, other scientists are working to clone animals that have become extinct more recently. One such animal is the Tasmanian tiger. The Tasmanian tiger, or thylacine is not really a tiger at all. It is more closely related to the kangaroo and opossum and actually looks like a dog that carried its young in a pouch. Thylacine killed many sheep belonging to English settlers to Australia in the 1800s. As a result, they were trapped, shot, and poisoned to extinction. The last one died in a Tasmanian zoo in 1936.

Though it was scorned while it lived, it is honored in death, and appears as a symbol on license plates, beverage labels and sporting gear. So it is perhaps fitting that cloning this animal from a baby that died 136 years ago and has been preserved in alcohol has become a goal of Australian scientists. Scott Weidensaul, writing in Audubon magazine explains how the Tasmanian tiger baby is at the center of a far ranging controversy: "But, now, 136 years after its death and 66 years after its species was declared extinct, the preserved baby sits at the junction of molecular biology, conservation ethics, and endangered species politics. That's a lot to pin to a dead creature you could easily cup in two hands."[25]

There are many obstacles to overcome, however, before a thylacine clone takes its first breath. Just like the wooly mammoth, well-preserved thylacine cells have not been found. While

*Some scientists are working to bring back the Tasmanian tiger, also known as a thylacine, which was declared extinct in 1936.*

some specimens have been preserved in alcohol, the DNA that scientists have extracted so far is incomplete. In order to clone a thylacine, scientists would have to fill in the missing pieces with DNA from other marsupials, hoping that the match would be close enough to function properly. Even if that were technically possible, some argue that finding a suitable surrogate would present an even greater hurdle, since the thylacine has no close living animal relatives.

Some conservationists object to using precious resources to clone a thylacine when so many other living species are currently endangered. Michael Lynch, the executive director of the Tasmanian Conservation Trust, does not mince words when he speaks about better use of the funds devoted to cloning a thylacine: "If somebody gave the Tasmanian Conservation Trust that amount of money, I could run 50 recovery programs, and with the people I could have at my disposal, I could guarantee a bloody good success rate. And these are species that are here now, that are being threatened."[26] In fact, reports of the thylacine's extinction may be premature. Reports of thylacine sightings in the wilds of Australia are not uncommon, though none have been confirmed so far.

One extinct animal with good future cloning prospects is the bucardo mountain goat, which became extinct when its last living member was killed by a falling tree in January 2000. Fortunately, before this native Spanish goat died, scientists extracted tissue from its ears since they anticipated the inevitable disappearance of the species. The cells are preserved in good condition, which should simplify the task of cloning the goat. However, unless scientists can create a male by artificially removing a chromosome, the future clones will all be females.

## Here Kitty Kitty Kitty!

Though scientists and conservationists use mostly the power of reason to promote the cloning of animals, it is pure emotion that drives many people to want to clone their pets. It is difficult to accept the loss of a beloved pet, and cloning promises that letting go might not be necessary after all. The first cloned cat—aptly named CC (CopyCat)—made his appearance in 2002. He was the first offspring of a company named Savings and Clone, which has since gone out of business. The company once offered to clone the cats of the first six owners who were willing to spend $50,000 for the privilege. Four people took them up on the offer.

Though he was a clone, CC's color differed from that of his genetic mother, a calico shorthair. The company attributed CC's fur color to the variations common among calico cats. Curt Youngs, an associate professor in the Animal Science Department of Iowa State University in Ames, Iowa, warned that CC's differences were predictable. Youngs explains, "I think people are going to be disappointed that Fluffy neither looks the same nor acts the same."[27] He also said that the conditions in which an animal is raised as well as the health and nutrition of the sur-

*The first cloned cat, named CopyCat, shown at 7-weeks-old in 2002. The death of a family pet can cause owners to consider cloning the lost animal.*

rogate mother contribute to an animal's disposition and even the texture of its coat.

Cats are not the only pets that have been cloned. Another company, owned by parent company Cyagra, which clones cattle and pigs, promises the possibility of cloning dogs and birds as well as cats. The company—PerPetuate—charges $890 dollars per clone, which includes one year of storage for a pet's DNA. Once the fee is paid, the owner's veterinarian receives instructions and materials from the company for collecting the

DNA samples. Pet owners are encouraged to plan ahead, since it is easier and more efficient to collect a DNA sample while the pet is still alive. The samples are then frozen and stored in Per-Petuate's bio-kennels until the owner is ready to clone the pet. PerPetuate's website includes a gallery of beloved pets whose DNA samples are stored in these bio-kennels awaiting the time when pet cloning becomes more technically and financially feasible.

Emotional attachment to a favorite pet is not the only justification for pet cloning. Advanced Cell Technologies, a leader in the animal cloning field, foresees cloning service animals such as search and rescue dogs and guide dogs for the blind. Since these dogs are often neutered at a young age to prevent problems associated with breeding, cloning offers another way to duplicate them. ACT explains its stance on cloning: "A good deal of a cat or dog's demeanor is thought to be genetically determined. Although one can argue that there are already plenty of cats and dogs in the world that need homes, people still use traditional breeding methods to try to reproduce a particularly desirable animal."[28] ACT has a research program that focuses on pets and service animals.

Demeanor and sweet temperament were behind the Reddell family's decision to clone their pet Brahma bull named Chance. They acquired the white bull when he was seven years old. His calm disposition was renowned, not only in Texas, where the Reddells live, but nationwide. Chance even appeared on the David Letterman Show. Schoolchildren were often photographed with the white bull, and the Reddells treated him like a beloved family member. As he aged, however, they worried that they would be devastated by his loss. So, when nearby Texas A&M University agreed to clone him, they were thrilled.

Ten months after Chance died in 1999 at the age of 21, his clone—Second Chance—was born. Though Second Chance looked identical to Chance, the clone's disposition was far different from that of his biological parent. Twice, Second Chance attacked his owner and seriously injured him—once when he was four and again when he was six. However, Ralph Reddell remained optimistic. He continued to believe that the clone would acquire Chance's calm disposition by the time he was seven, the age at which they had acquired Second Chance's gentle genetic parent.

Possible differences in coat color and temperament are not the only criticisms of pet cloning. The Humane Society of the United States, an animal protection group, points to the four million animals that are put to death each year because they cannot find homes. The Humane Society encourages people who lose a pet to adopt another from a local animal shelter. Currently, no federal or state legislation is proposed to regulate pet cloning, and associations of veterinarians have not expressed official stances on the issue.

As cloning technology improves, people from various interest groups consider how to use it to further their agendas. Each possible application of cloning has its proponents and its critics. Ideas are argued in many forums: newspapers and magazines, television talk shows, meetings and scientific journals, living rooms, and voting booths as people vote for politicians who support their own positions. As various groups put forth their views, the public absorbs these arguments, and eventually public opinion is realized in the form of legislation and court decisions. Ultimately, society funds the science that meets its approval. The jury on cloning animals is still out.

# CHAPTER 4

# MAKING BABIES

Every discussion about different applications of cloning converges on the ethics of human cloning. The birth of Louise Brown in 1978, the first test-tube baby, forced society to confront the question of whether or not it is moral to "fool mother nature." While many scientists believe that it is only a matter of time until a human baby is cloned—indeed, some claim that it has already happened—theologians, ethicists, politicians, and many public citizens condemn the possibility. Some believe that society must pass anti-cloning laws in order to respect human life, while others ask, "Who would be harmed?" and believe that the fears about cloning are irrational and overblown.

## NATURE VS. NURTURE

"People say that cloning means that if a child dies, you can get that child back. It's heart wrenching. You could never get that child back. It would be something different. People are not genes. They are so much more than that."

—Ian Wilmut

Quoted in Michael Specter with Gina Kolata, "After Decades of Missteps, How Cloning Succeeded," New York Times, March 3, 1997, http://query.nytimes.com/gst/fullpage.html?sec=health&res=9A04E0D71F31F930A35750C0A961958260

## Is it Possible to Clone a Human?

The birth of the cloned sheep Dolly was a pivotal moment in the history of reproductive science. While the cloning of frogs in the 1960s preceded Dolly's cloning, she was the first reported successful clone of an adult mammal. This event unleashed speculation around the world that cloning humans would quickly follow.

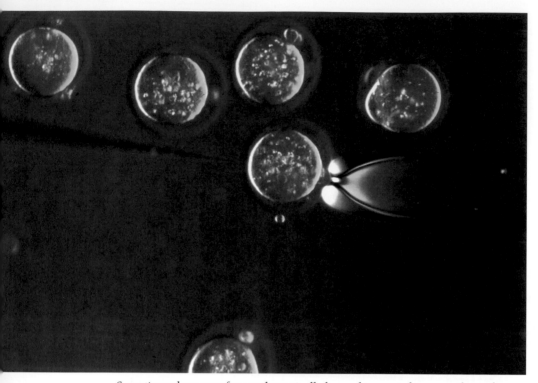

*Somatic nuclear transfer can theoretically be used to create human embryos from stem cells that are harvested.*

Many of the actual techniques involved in transferring the nucleus of a cell, which contains its DNA, to an egg that has been emptied of its own nucleus are already widely practiced with animals. There has been a virtual parade of cloned mammals since Dolly made her debut: cattle, pigs, goats, mice, horses, dogs, cats, and monkeys have all been successfully cloned. The same process—known as somatic nuclear transfer—can theoretically be used to create human embryos from which stem cells are harvested. This is known as therapeutic cloning, since the stem cells are used therapeutically to treat diseases or injuries. It is highly controversial, however, since many people see it as one step further down the slippery slope toward reproductive cloning.

Reproductive cloning begins in exactly the same way. The end result, however, is a fully formed, living, breathing baby that is the genetic twin of the individual who donates the cell nucleus. "Repugnant" is a word that people often use to describe their horror at the prospect of cloning a human. Discussions about human cloning often refer to Dr. Frankenstein, the fictional doctor who concocted a monster in his laboratory from human parts. Though there is widespread mistrust of the motivations of those who would clone a human, scientists are becoming increasingly adept at the genetic manipulations involved.

Lack of scientific expertise will not be the stumbling block that prevents human cloning, since it is already technically possible. The only way to prevent human cloning will be through laws that make it illegal, lack of funding, and complete agreement among all members of society that science has reached a boundary over which it must not cross.

## Religious Views

That boundary is one that inspires passionate debate among religious leaders. Many point to the Bible to support their opinions on cloning. In some cases, they use the same Bible story to illustrate their thinking even though their interpretations differ radically. Gina Kolata, a science writer for the *New York Times* tells how one Catholic priest, Albert Moraczewski, cites the story in the Book of Genesis about Adam and Eve in which God gives humans powers over all the other creatures of the earth. In her book *Clone,* Kolata relays Moraczewski's interpretation of that story: "Adam and Eve were given freedom in the garden but with one limitation—they were not to eat from the tree of knowledge of good and evil—which, if disobeyed, would lead to death. Accordingly, human beings have been granted intelligence and free will so that they can search for, and recognize the truth and freely pursue the good."[29] Moraczewski continues to explain that cloning ventures beyond the powers that God intended for humans, and that cloning a child interferes with both the identity of the child and the natural act of creating one.

However, Kolata also tells of an orthodox Jewish rabbi, Moshe Tendler, who refers to the same passage, but interprets it in a very different way. According to the rabbi, Adam and Eve purposefully ate from the tree that endows them with the ability to decide what is good and what is evil. "It would not be in character with the Jewish tradition to have a technology that could have outcomes that are good—like preserving the family line of a Holocaust survivor who had no other living relatives—and decide, ahead of time, not to use it for fear of its evil consequences."[30] Both religious leaders addressed a presidential commission that was formed shortly after Dolly's birth to make recommendations about cloning.

Other religions also weigh in on the cloning debate. Leading U.S. Islamic scholar Dr. Abdulaziz Sachedina, believes Muslims would support cloning if it helps parents in committed relationships have children. Some Baptist and Methodist church leaders worry that cloning research might unfairly favor the most affluent members of society due to the considerable expense of this technology. Buddhists have still another perspective on cloning. Since Buddhists do not accept the Western view of individuality, they are less concerned with the process by which children are created. According to an MSNBC story about religious views on cloning,

> Cloning can even be viewed as a tool for reaching enlightenment, or liberation from the world of suffering. The Dalai Lama once said hypothetically that he would welcome creation of a person who had all good human qualities and no bad qualities, because it would facilitate the process of rebirth and liberation. On the other hand, some Buddhist monks believe that cloning is just a foolhardy attempt to eliminate suffering from the world.[31]

Native American tribes also express varied perspectives on cloning. Some regard cloning as disruptive to the natural order and balance in nature. Other Native American leaders see the

Time *magazine highlighted human cloning in November 1993, addressing both the possible benefits, safety concerns, as well as the moral and religious reservations about the process.*

technology as one way to ensure the survival of some native peoples whose populations have almost entirely disappeared.

## Is Cloning Safe?

Lack of safety is often cited to criticize cloning. Healthy live births are the exception rather than the rule in cloning. Dolly herself was the sole successful outcome of 277 attempts. Even biotechnology companies that clone sheep, cows, and pigs admit that their success rate is very low. Most agree that it still takes about 100 cow eggs to produce one or two cloned cows. However, many point out that even natural conception might be considered unsafe if measured by the same standards. Most reproductive biologists agree that a very high percentage of naturally fertilized eggs fail to result in pregnancy. Studies prove that many of those failed pregnancies are due to genetic defects.

### HUMAN CLONING BAN

"Human cloning is deeply troubling to me, and to most Americans. Life is a creation, not a commodity. Our children are gifts to be loved and protected, not products to be designed and manufactured."

—President George W. Bush.

Quoted in White House Press Release, "President Bush Calls on Senate to Back Human Cloning Ban," April 10, 2002. http://www.whitehouse.gov/news/releases/2002/04/print/200220410-4.html

Moreover, even a problem-free, natural pregnancy does not guarantee a perfect baby. Many babies are born with genetic diseases and abnormalities or birth defects. In fact, Douglas Melton, the director of Harvard's Stem Cell Institute ponders how society might view cloning babies once the technology improves: "I'm not saying this will really happen, but let's say 20 years from now, the failure rate is below what you and I call the 'natural birth' rate. Here's the puzzle. Would the government then be justified in telling the population you can no longer create children by what you and I call 'natural childbirth,' because the probability of defect is higher than it is by cloning?"[32]

*Harvard scientist Stephen J. Gould noted the many ways that twins, like clones, can differ from each other even though they begin with identical DNA.*

Melton acknowledges that this scenario is unlikely in the fore-seeable future as cloning still has many unknowns. About 30 percent of clones are born with a condition called "large off-spring syndrome," and must be delivered surgically. Scientists do not know why many cloned animals die prematurely from infections and other complications. In addition, no one knows how cloning might affect the sensitive mechanisms responsible for mood and other aspects of human mental health.

## The Mental Health of Clones: Living Up to the DNA?

In fact, most of the objections to cloning focus on the trauma inherent in the clone's knowledge that he or she is not unique—that, in fact, a clone's very origin is the result of a deliberate attempt to duplicate someone else. While all parents have dreams for their children, cloned children might feel especially pressured to live up to their parent's expectations. Parents who choose to clone a great athlete or musician would necessarily expect their child to accomplish great athletic feats or possess a natural flair for music.

One of the primary concerns voiced by the President's Council on Bioethics in 2002 chaired by Dr. Leon R. Kass, in fact was this: "Living up to parental hopes and expectations is frequently a burden for children; it could be a far greater burden for a cloned individual. The shadow of the cloned child's original might be hard for the child to escape as would parental attitudes that sought in the child's very existence to replicate, imitate, or replace the original."[33] The Council's report emphasizes the constant scrutiny that a clone might endure. Clones might not even receive credit for their own achievements. Anticipating comparisons between clones and twins, the report points out that since twins are born at the same time, they do not face the burden of trying to match the achievements of someone who has already lived a full life. These expectations would be particularly burdensome if a child were cloned from a dead relative or a sibling who had succumbed to illness.

Others point to the differences between identical twins to prove that a person's nature is not purely genetic in origin. Stephen J. Gould (1941–2002), a well-known Harvard scientist who often wrote about complex issues in science noted the many ways that twins differ from each other even though they begin with identical DNA. He pointed out that twins begin life with more in common than do clones. They begin with the same DNA. They are exposed to the same prenatal environment, have the same parents, and live in a common time and place.

Even so, twins usually differ remarkably from one another in personality and achievements. Gould referred to famous conjoined twins such as Chang and Eng, who lived in the 19th century, as an example. One was moody and morose, the other cheerful and optimistic. Most people agree that attitudes, moods, and personality are such a complex mix of factors that it is impossible to reduce them to genetic factors alone. Those who support human cloning research tend to emphasize the impact of environment on a person's destiny. They point out that parents must always adapt their expectations to the reality of their children. Those who oppose cloning fear that a clone would lead a life inevitably filled with disappointment and frustration.

## Are You My Mother? The Legal Complications of Cloning

In addition to the questions about the potential psychological harm of being a clone, another interesting question concerns a clone's parentage. Before the advent of assisted reproduction, the woman who gave birth to a baby was inarguably its biological mother. Cloning, however, complicates the issue. Is the mother the egg donor, the nucleus donor, or the surrogate? Who decides?

In 1987, a New Jersey housewife agreed to become pregnant through artificial insemination and then give the resulting baby to the couple whose husband was the biological father. But she changed her mind. She was, she argued, the baby's biological mother, since her egg was fertilized with donor sperm. A bitter custody battle followed, but the courts finally ruled against her.

The courts would have to navigate a complicated genetics trail to sort out the identity of a clone's biological—and legal—parents. Some might argue that the legal parents are the couple that arranges to clone the child. Others might single out the donor of the nucleus, the egg donor, or even the natural parents of the nucleus donor, since ultimately they provided the clone's DNA. Or it is possible that someone, whose own eggs are damaged, might select a donor with favorable genetic qualities, clone that person, implant the embryo in her own uterus and give birth to a bouncing baby clone nine months later. Is she then the clone's mother? Some might argue the point.

When two lesbian partners decided to have a baby in San Francisco, California, they both wanted to be part of the baby's biological heritage. They used artificial insemination to fertilize the egg from one woman, and implanted it in the uterus of the second woman, who gave birth to resulting twin girls. However, when the relationship ended in 2004, custody of the twins was granted to the birth mother, even though she was not the twins' biological mother. These complicated legal issues will inevitably inspire heated debate in the future if and when cloning human babies becomes a reality.

## Famous and Infamous Clones

The announcement of Dolly's birth unleashed a torrent of speculation about whether or not a human baby clone would soon follow. However, Dolly's birth announcement was not the first time that the arrival of a cloned baby ignited public sentiment. Twenty years before Dolly respected science writer David Rorvik

# Cloning A Man: Fact or Fiction

David Rorvik, a science writer, told the world about the strange events that unfolded when an eccentric millionaire named Max asked him to help in his quest to clone himself. Rorvik's tale was published in 1978 in a book entitled *In His Image. The Cloning of a Man*. Readers accompany Rorvik as he meets Max, searches for a doctor—Darwin—who carries out the experiment, and helps Max select a surrogate named Sparrow to give birth to the clone. Finally, Rorvik describes his feelings as he gazes at the new family: "Sparrow said that she wished the baby had come at Christmas—still two weeks away. Max was delighted that it had happened in 1976—his contribution to the Bicentennial, he said. Darwin was beaming. Max was sitting on the edge of Sparrow's bed. She was holding the baby in a small blanket to her breast. It was not, I thought, exactly the nuclear family. But it was a thrilling sight, this old man, this young girl, this strange baby. I wondered what this wrinkled little creature could see. I wondered what he might know. I wondered if he would be brave."

David Rorvik, *In His Image the Cloning of a Man.* Philadelphia: J.B. Lippincott Company, 1978, pg. 205

*David Rorvik, right, author of* In His Image: the Cloning of a Man, *appeared on the* Today *show in 1978 to defend his book's claim that a person had been cloned.*

published an account of a mysterious millionaire—code named 'Max'—who asked him to help in his quest to clone himself.

Rorvik's book was published in 1978. Entitled *In His Image, the Cloning of a Man*, it recounts Rorvik's supposed meetings with 'Max,' his quest for a willing scientist, to whom he gave the pseudonym 'Darwin,' to carry out the cloning experiment, and the reasons that the surrogate—Sparrow—agreed to become pregnant with the clone. At the time, many people did not believe the story. No one ever met the resulting clone. But Rorvik, whose reputation for scientific reporting was unblemished, insisted that the story was true.

Many scientists were outraged. People often react with fear and suspicion when new scientific findings are revealed, and a report that a scientist had secretly cloned a person was exactly the type of publicity that scientists hope to avoid. Though many scientists refused to speak out in order to avoid promoting the book, others were quick to dismiss Rorvik's claim. They insisted that the technology to clone a person did not exist and that the cloning technique described by Rorvik was based on the procedure used to clone frogs in the 1960s and would not work in mammals. In the end, a British scientist whose work Rorvik referred to in the book successfully sued the author and publisher. When Rorvik refused to provide concrete evidence that the clone existed, a court ruled that his book was a hoax.

No one ever figured out why Rorvik risked his reputation in this way, but the incident did bring human cloning to the forefront of public discussion. Some scientists, though they insisted they did not believe the story, were determined to make sure that human cloning never happened. Three molecular biologists, using the Freedom of Information Act, forced the government to disclose any grants awarded for cloning research. Jonathan Beckwith, a molecular biologist from Harvard spoke for many when he said, "Even if this is a hoax, there is a good chance that human cloning is not too far off. Some public discussion should take place. We'll wake up one day. Maybe it's not happened this time. But next time or the time after that, we'll find that we really have created a monster we didn't intend to create."[34]

Rorvik's book became a best-seller, even though many scorned it. Moreover, the reactions of both scientists and the press fed into a general growing mistrust of science. As Kolata points out in her book *Clone:* "Many fear that scientists will secretly, or not so secretly, clone a human being, whether or not it is legal and whether or not the public approves."[35] Scientists who oppose the idea of cloning a person urged that science impose a voluntary restriction on research that could culminate in human cloning. As the rushing tide of research into genetics became a groundswell in the 1970s, many scientists joined the public to insist that science not cross boundaries into areas reserved for the divine.

The story of Max, Darwin, and Sparrow finally faded, but it was not the last time that a human cloning hoax was born. In 2003, a company called Clonaid claimed to have cloned a human on behalf of the Raelians, a new age sect founded in 1997 by a former French journalist known as "Rael."

Rael said he was a direct descendant of aliens who created human life on earth by cloning. A spokesperson for the group held a press conference to announce the birth and claimed that the seven-pound baby girl named 'Eve' was healthy and beautiful. At the same press conference, the spokesperson revealed that several more Raelian clones were due in the following few months. However, the Raelians never introduced the clones to the public and both scientists and the public were skeptical. Robert Lanza from Advanced Cell Technologies, a leader in the animal cloning field, says of the claim: "Without any scientific data, one has to be very, very skeptical. This is a group again that has no scientific track record, never published a single, sci-

# Etiquette of Entertaining a Clone

The public was fascinated by cloning in the 1970s. The New York Times published these humorous questions and answers written by columnist Russell Baker in 1978:

**"Q: If a clone comes to my house for dinner, how should I treat him?**

A: Do not open the conversation with some graceless remark such as 'I hear you're a clone.' Many clones do not know they are clones and might be disturbed to hear it from a stranger. If they have been told, they may introduce the subject themselves with some offhand remark such as 'You know, of course, I'm a clone.' Some self-disparaging remark,

such as 'You're lucky, I'm a clod,' might put the clone at ease. Under no circumstances should you tell a clone joke."

**"Q: I'd like to be cloned, but am afraid. Is it painful?**

A: Not at all. You simply peel off one little tiny cell from your person, place it in a female human egg cell, and place the mixture in the reproductive housing of an obliging woman. In nine months she will convert it into a clone and send it to you."

Russell Baker, "So You're Thinking of Cloning," *New York Times*, May 11, 1978, pg. 23.

entific paper in this area."[36] At about the same time, Dr. Panos Zavos, a former professor from the University of Kentucky also announced a cloned baby in progress. And an Italian doctor, Severino Antinori claimed that three of his patients were due to deliver clones in the near future. None of these cloning reports was ever confirmed.

The latest cloning scandal to rock the science world embarrassed the highly respected journal *Science* in 2005. *Science*, like most journals sends papers that are being considered for pub-

*Claude Vorilhon, also known as Rael, claims he was the direct descendant of aliens who created life on earth by cloning.*

lication to outside experts who then recommend that the paper either be published or rejected. In this case, a South Korean scientist, Hwang Woo Suk of Seoul National University, claimed that he had cloned a human embryo from an adult cell and extracted its stem cells in his research lab in South Korea. Three outside reviewers approved the paper for publication, and it was rushed to press.

When it appeared on May 12, 2005, it was met with great excitement. Dr. Hwang was invited to lecture around the world about his work, and many scientists visited his lab to witness the cloning process described in his paper. However, within six months, one of the paper's co-authors admitted that photographs of the supposed cloned cells were fraudulent. Laurie Zoloth, director of the Center for Bioethics, Science and Society at Northwestern University in Chicago describes the troubling questions that arise when something like this occurs in a realm that people trust: "Did we see only what we yearned to see?"[37] she asks. Hwang was ultimately dismissed from the University of Seoul for publishing fraudulent data and for obtaining women's eggs unethically from his own female researchers.

## FRAUD ALERT

"Scientists, ethicists and others said that it can be almost impossible to detect a well-crafted scientific deception—at least at first—but added that greater safeguards are worth considering in the aftermath of the Korean scandal."

Rick Weiss, "Stem Cell Fraud Worries U.S. Scientists," *Washington Post*, December 24, 2005. Washingtonpost.com/wp-dyn/content/article/2005/12/23/AR2005122301518_pf

The technology already exists to clone a human, and many people believe that it is highly likely that a human baby will be cloned from an adult some day. When reputable scientists confirm the cloning and are able to duplicate the process, the event will be widely publicized, celebrated by some and denounced by others. Historically, great advances in science are always viewed with suspicion and doubt at first. Ted Koppel, a well-known commentator, makes the point on the video entitled *Why Not*

*South Korea stem cell scientist Hwang Woo-Suk claimed that he had cloned a human embryo from an adult cell and extracted its stem cells. Hwang's claim was false and he was dismissed from his university for publishing fraudulent data.*

*Clone a Human,* "In fact, if we spent our lives worrying about the impact of unforeseen consequences, we'd never get anything done. We'd be paralyzed. And if we permit ourselves to be influenced by the first or second or even third round of concerns produced by each new development, we'd almost certainly end up worrying about the wrong things."[38]

While many groups profess grave concern about the consequences of human cloning, history confirms that, with few exceptions, most scientists want their research to serve the best interests of society. The worst outcomes are almost never realized. It is probably impossible to prevent human cloning from moving forward, and it is important to be responsible about human cloning when it happens.

# THE FUTURE
# OF CLONING

The beginning of the 21st century is an exciting time for molecular biology. Scientists steadily focus ever more closely on the smallest mechanisms of life. The more intense the focus, the more likely they will learn how to control those mechanisms. Science now teeters on the brink of cloning a human being.

Decisions about cloning in the 21st century hinge more on ethicists, religious leaders, politicians, and the public than they do on science. These groups ultimately make the decisions about how cloning research is funded and how far society will allow this research to progress. In general, great scientific advances begin in the laboratory and then find practical applications in the everyday world. Often, those applications are unexpected. When James Watson and Francis Crick announced the double helix structure of the DNA molecule in 1953, for example, no one realized until much later that DNA could help catch criminals.

## "A TRICKY WAY TO MAKE A LAMB"

"Ten years after the announcement of Dolly's creation, cloning is a subject that still scares most of us when all it really is is a new, very difficult, very inefficient, and very tricky way to make a lamb." Arthur Caplan, Ph.D., director of the Center for Bioethics at the University of Pennsylvania.

Arthur Caplan, "10 Years After Dolly: Clones, Crooks, and Crazies," MSNBC.com, February 22, 2007. http://www.msnbc.msn.com/id/18136717/

Cloning, on the other hand, has followed a different course. Human biologists mostly abandoned cloning technology after the 1960s. Instead scientists who specialized in animals and agriculture studied cloning in hopes of improving their products. Instead of the neat, sterile world of the laboratory, cloning's headline events occurred in the noisy, smelly world of the barnyard. Now the public must wrestle with the issues raised by cloning. Some believe that the science must proceed and trust that the dilemmas will be resolved. Others insist that cloning is leading society down a dangerous path and must be stopped before it is too late to turn back.

## Designer Babies

One issue that frequently arises is to what extent society is prepared to allow physicians and parents to manipulate the genes of unborn children. The video produced by ABC News entitled *Why Not Clone a Human?* suggests that rich parents might clone several embryos when they decide to have a child. They could then manipulate the genes to improve their child's looks, intelligence, or talents, and implant the best embryos back into the mother until she delivers the resulting clone. This privilege would naturally be reserved for those who could afford it, since reproductive intervention is expensive.

The video makes the point that cloning would exaggerate the gap between the rich and the poor. In addition, the video poses the question of who might be eliminated if people could design their children in this way. Mark Trumbino, a dwarf, asks in the video: "Who are we prepared to lose? Are we prepared to love whatever we get?"[39] Trumbino assumes that children with the genetic abnormality that results in dwarfism would be among those that might never be born if parents had a choice.

The social policy of selecting desired genetic traits is known as eugenics and is often associated with Nazi abuses during World War II (1939–1945). Twenty years after the end of World War II, however, the idea of improving the human species by selecting specific genetic traits was still discussed. J.B.S. Haldane, a British biologist, addressed a meeting of scientists in the 1960s saying,

> The cloning of humans would become possible and
> could be a tremendous boon, enabling humans to con-

*Demonstrators outside of a biotech firm hold signs with a Nazi swastika, implying a link between cloning and the policy of eugenics practiced by the Nazis in World War II.*

trol their own evolution. Of course we would clone the best and the brightest, probably waiting until people were at least fifty, and had demonstrated their superiority, before cloning them. Thus we would gradually increase the number of great thinkers, great artists, great athletes, even great beauties in the population.[40]

Most modern thinkers are horrified by the concept of eugenics, but once again, the line between the acceptable and the unacceptable is unclear. Today, prenatal tests determine whether or not a fetus has a genetic disorder. This knowledge enables parents to decide whether or not to carry that baby to term. In some countries, where boy babies are preferred over girls, technicians with portable ultrasound machines travel from town to town to determine the sex of pregnant women's babies. Women often terminate their pregnancies if their unborn child's sex is not the one they want. The procedures involved in cloning would give parents that same knowledge and force them to make the same decisions.

## Which Comes First... the Egg?

While many people voice concern about genetic selection, one fact about cloning remains constant. So far, cloning still entails transferring a nucleus from an adult cell to an egg that has had its own nucleus removed. Scientists acknowledge that the success rate is low, which makes large scale cloning of animals or humans currently impractical. When the nuclei from the skin cells of cows are transferred into cow eggs, 98 percent of those cow eggs never develop. That failure rate is a major obstacle.

### MIRACLE OR ABOMINATION?

"Many people wonder if this is a miracle for which we can thank God, or an ominous new way to play God ourselves. At the very least, it represents the ongoing tension between faith and science." Nancy Duff, theologian at Princeton Theological Seminary.

Quoted in Kolata, *Clone,* pg. 18.

Many people worry that poor women would risk their health to sell eggs for needed income. This concern has united strong pro-life and pro-choice forces around the world that are usually in opposition. According to an article in the online version of the *San Francisco Chronicle,* the threat to women's health is a primary reason that human cloning is banned in many countries. Nigel Cameron, a bioethics adviser, explains why he favors that ban: "When apologists for therapeutic cloning speak airily of hopes of cures, not only are they guilty of hype, they fail to disclose that every single cloning effort requires eggs. These eggs are not laid by chickens. They must be extracted, after more than a week of powerful daily hormone injections, by inserting

*Scientists acknowledge that the success rate for cloning is low, which makes large scale cloning of animals or humans impractical.*

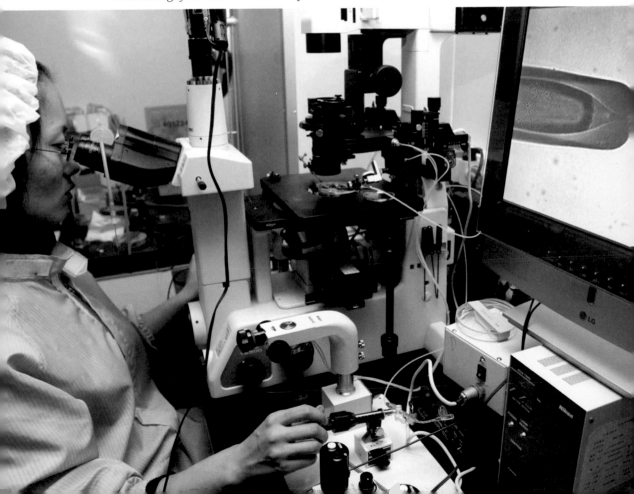

a needle into a woman's ovary."[41] Cameron is a trained minister and dean of a Christian worldview think tank in Washington, DC.

Cameron also points to the recent case of South Korean scientist Hwang Woo Suk to underscore the necessity of international standards for human research. One factor in Hwang's disgrace was his admission that he obtained eggs from two junior members of his research team. Scientists all over the world follow guidelines that forbid senior scientists from endangering the people who work under them. Hwang's use of these eggs is exactly the situation these guidelines are intended to prevent.

The high failure rate of nuclear transfer is a problem that scientists believe they can overcome. They are optimistic that, as they become more proficient at transferring nuclei from one cell to another, and further their understanding of how the egg itself affects embryo development, the failure rate will diminish. Researchers know that a chemical process within the egg is responsible for reprogramming the transferred nucleus and causing it to act as if it were undifferentiated.

Lee Silver, an ethicist from Princeton University, believes that it may be possible one day to bypass the egg altogether, which would make the debate over procuring eggs irrelevant. Silver describes the work of two researchers at the University of Pennsylvania who reported in 2003 that they had discovered how to trick a mouse's embryonic stem cells into forming miniature ovaries that ovulate normal mouse eggs. Silver explains: "If the same process can be performed for use with available human embryonic stem cells, it would become possible to produce unlimited numbers of human eggs in a petri dish without any need for donors or sellers."[42] The research on human applications for this technology, however, is many years away.

## Cloning Policies in the United States

Restrictions on human research of any type in the United States remain one of the primary reasons that this research moves so slowly in this country. The FDA, the U.S government agency that regulates both human and animal cloning, is legally bound to disregard social, political, or moral arguments when making decisions. However, there are many powerful interest groups in the United States. The biotechnology industry and groups that oppose abortion both actively lobby Congress to pass laws that favor their positions. As a result, the U.S. severely restricts federal funding of this research, but does not prohibit cloning outright.

In June 2007, the U.S. House of Representatives joined the U.S. Senate and voted to ease federal restrictions on stem cell research from embryos discarded by fertility clinics. Perhaps anticipating that President George W. Bush would veto the legislation, Speaker of the House Nancy Pelosi, a Democrat from California said, "Science is a gift of God to all of us and science has taken us to a place that is biblical in its power to cure. And that is the embryonic stem cell research."[43] This legislation was intended to overturn Bush's 2001 order prohibiting the use of federal money for research on new stem cell lines.

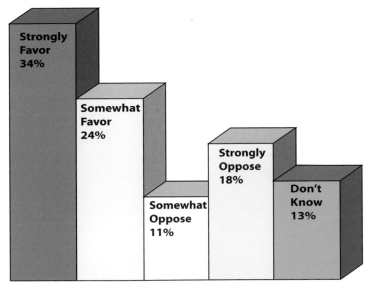

# Public Opinion on Embryonic Stem Cell Research

*Research!America, Available online at: http://www.researchamerica.org/ polldata/2005/stemcell(parade).pdf*

Despite widespread public approval of stem cell research, President Bush vetoed the measure saying, "Destroying human life in the hopes of saving human life is not ethical. The United States is a nation founded on the principle that all human life is sacred."[44] This was the second time President Bush used his veto power to overturn legislation to allow federal funding of stem cell research. Advocates for this research hope that the next President is more supportive. Democrats are united in support of stem cell research, while Republican support is divided.

Some states have taken the matter into their own legislative hands to bypass federal restrictions. Maryland, New Jersey, and Connecticut have authorized state funding for human stem cell research. South Dakota, on the other hand, bans all embryonic

# Opposing Arguments

In 2001 President George W. Bush issued an order that prohibited the use of federal money for research on new stem cell lines derived from embryos. Many scientists expressed concern that existing stem cell lines were damaged or inadequate for their research. In the ensuing five years, Congress debated the advantages and disadvantages of stem cell research. Finally in 2007, the U.S. House of Representatives joined the U.S. Senate and approved legislation to overturn Bush's 2001 order. Polls show that a majority of Americans support embryonic stem cell research. The statements of two Representatives sum up the opposing arguments. Representative Mike Pence an Indiana Republican says, "I believe that life begins at conception and destroying embryonic human life for the purpose of research is morally wrong." Representative Christopher Murphy, a Connecticut Democrat counters: "Being pro-life is about more than caring for the unborn. It's about caring for the living as well." President Bush vetoed the legislation.

(Source: Jeff Zeleny, "House Votes to Expand Stem Cell Research," *New York Times,* June 8, 2007, pg. A23.)

*In June 2007, the U.S. House of Representatives and the Senate voted to ease
federal restrictions on stem cell research from embryos discarded by fertility
clinics. Despite widespread public approval, President Bush vetoed the measure.*

stem cell research and threatens scientists who engage in therapeutic cloning with criminal prosecution.

While some state lawmakers have qualms about this research, academic institutions and biotechnology companies point out that stem cell research can be an economic boon to the states that allow it. An editorial in the *New York Times* explains why Wisconsin Democratic Governor Jim Doyle planned to veto legislation that banned cloning in his state: "That Legislation would have made therapeutic cloning a criminal offense punishable by up to 10 years in jail. He has instead embarked on a drive to recruit stem cell companies for Wisconsin, with a goal of capturing 10 percent of the stem cell industry by 2015."[45] The editorial emphasizes how unfair it is to rely on a small number of states to assume the entire burden of this research. It further points out that people who live in states that ban therapeutic cloning would not refuse lifesaving therapies developed in other states.

California is one state that took the debate straight to the voters. In 2004, Californians approved Proposition 71 that authorizes $3 billion dollars in state funds to finance embryonic stem cell research. Court challenges to that proposition have

*While many lawmakers have doubts about stem cell research, support from the people in their districts can make a difference.*

been overcome, and the money is being distributed to research facilities around the state. California's investment in stem cell research is by far the most extensive in the country and has begun attracting many of the top researchers in the field.

## Cloning Policies Around the World

While policy in this country varies from state to state, many countries such as China, Great Britain, India, Sweden, and Israel actively support stem cell research. The Singapore government will fund a $400 million dollar complex devoted to stem cell research alone to accommodate up to 2000 scientists. Top foreign students being trained in the United States often return to their own countries, where research in stem cell treatments for disease and injury is encouraged. Patients in these countries are treated quickly with the newest discoveries. International competition to discover cures and drug therapies that use stem cells is keen. Dr. Evan Snyder, who runs the embryonic stem cell research program at the Burnham Institute in La Jolla, California explains how the importance of this research inspires scientists around the world: "For the first time, we have a lot of competition...I don't think we've had as much concern for another country besting us in science since the race to the moon."[46]

While many opponents of stem cell research are troubled by the destruction of any embryo, some countries, such as Canada and Australia, permit stem cell research on discarded embryos from fertility clinics. Germany and Norway ban all human cloning. South Korea, the home of the disgraced scientist Hwang Woo Suk, actively supports cloning research. In fact, before the world learned of the source of the eggs Hwang used in his research and he was forced to resign, more than 1000 Korean women volunteered to donate their own eggs for his research.

## Adult Stem Cells Show Limited Promise

Cases such as that of the South Korean scientist add fuel to the fierce opposition by religious conservatives and abortion opponents to any research that involves human embryos. Jeremy Rifkin, president of the Foundation on Economic Trends in

Washington, D.C. represents a coalition of 300 religious and ethics organizations that proposes a worldwide ban on human cloning. Rifkin suggests that scientists who clone human embryos should be punished with the same severity as rapists, murderers, and child abusers.

In fact, at the same time President Bush vetoed the stem cell legislation in 2007, he issued an executive order intended to promote what he and many others believe to be ethical stem cell research. That research focuses on adult stem cells. Adult stem cells are found in limited supply in various parts of the body including the brain, blood, and bone marrow. They differ from embryonic stem cells in that they have already begun to specialize. Scientists hope to discover a way to reverse this process and overcome the adult stem cell's destiny in the body. There have been some successes. Adult stem cells are used to treat a wide range of blood disorders and problems with the human immune system. Neural stem cells found in the brain have been injected into the spinal fluid of paralyzed rodents resulting in some restored movement.

Although adult stem cells seem to offer an alternative to stem cells from cloned embryos, drawbacks remain. The supply of adult stem cells in the body is limited and they are difficult to access. Also, unlike embryonic stem cells, adult stem cells have begun to show signs of the damage from ageing. Moreover, adult stem cells—unlike embryonic stem cells—do not seem to have the potential to become any of the 220 cell types in the human body.

And yet, if the problems can be overcome, adult stem cells may help cure diseases and rebuild organs without the ethical dilemmas posed by cloning. Arlene Klotzko, a science writer in England explains why scientists are excited about this research: "If scientists could transform a patient's adult stem cells into the cells needed to cure disease or damage, we could have our very own body repair kit without the need for therapeutic cloning. There is a lot at stake and we are still at the beginning of a long and very exciting journey."[47] While embryonic stem cell research is relatively new, scientists have been studying adult

*South Korea is one of the few countries that actively supports cloning research, which can often cause protestors to speak out against the government's policies.*

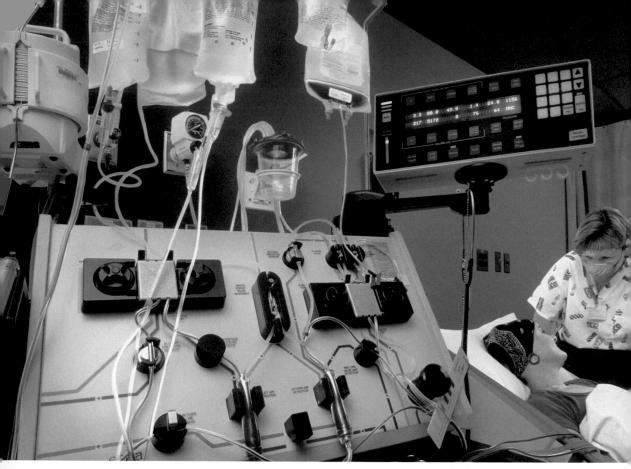

*A woman in an apheresis session, which collects stem cells. The supply of adult stem cells in the body is limited and collecting cells can be a painful and complicated process.*

stem cells for over forty years. No funding accompanied Bush's executive order.

Many scientists believe that adult stem cell research and embryonic stem cell research are both important. Professor Stephen Livesey, the Chief Executive Officer for the Australian Stem Cell Centre explains: "Adult and embryonic stem cell research should be done in parallel. For they are both stem cells and what we learn in one area will be of benefit to the other. They have very different characteristics, scientific challenges, potential application and research uses. One should not be excluded in preference for the other."[48] Some scientists are frustrated at what they believe to be shortsighted views of politicians, who vote on complex scientific issues that they do not fully understand.

## It May Be in the Genes

In June 2007 a possible solution to the embryonic versus adult stem cell debate made headlines around the world. Scientists have known for a long time that the egg has an important role in reprogramming an adult nucleus back to its embryonic state. The nucleus of a skin cell, for example, becomes capable of changing into any cell in the body once it is transferred into an egg. But while they knew *that* it happened, they had never figured out exactly how it happened. However, Shinya Yamanaka of Kyoto University in Japan announced in June 2007 that he has isolated four individual genes he believes are responsible for reprogramming skin cells back to their pre-differentiated states.

### SCIENCE VS. FAITH

"President Bush's veto of the embryonic stem cell bill is but another example of his disdain for science, his insistence on imposing fundamental religious views on everyone, and his indifference to the potential health benefits of embryonic stem cell research." Edd Doerr, President, Americans for Religious Liberty.

Letter to the Editor, *New York Times*, June 22, 2007, pg. A22.

The reaction of Irving Weissman, a leading stem cell biologist at Stanford University reflects that of many scientists, "From the point of view of moving biomedicine and regenerative medicine faster, this is about as big a deal as you could imagine."[49] Cell biologists around the world echo Weissman's excitement. When Dr. Yamanaka first reported his progress in 2006, two teams of scientists at other academic institutions embarked on studies to repeat and refine Dr. Yamanaka's results. In articles published in June 2007 in both *Nature* and *Cell-Stem Cell*, leading scientific journals, the three teams agreed that injecting the four genes into the skin cells of mice causes them to revert to cells that behave exactly like embryonic stem cells.

Though this development has the potential to end entirely the debate about cloning embryos to treat disease and injury, many hurdles remain before the technology is applied to humans. Scientists are confident, however, that future applications for humans are promising. Moreover, they are not alone in hoping that arguments concerning the moral status of an embryo will then be irrelevant. If embryonic-like stem cells can be created without eggs, most people would not consider the resulting cells different from other cells in the body. Richard Doerflinger, the spokesman on stem cells for the United States Conference of Catholic Bishops explains: "[This technique] raises no serious moral problem, because it creates embryonic-like stem cells without creating, harming, or destroying human lives at any stage. In themselves, embryonic stem cells have no moral status."[50] He further explains that the Catholic Bishops' objections to embryonic stem cell research rest solely on the resulting destruction of human embryos.

## Pro or Con—The Answers Depend on the Questions

As the debate about cloning and other genetic manipulations rage, many ethicists note that people's opinions vary according to the ways in which the questions are posed. After World War II, the world was horrified to learn of the eugenics movement in which one race was considered superior to others and people of the so-called inferior races were oppressed and even murdered.

### MAD SCIENTISTS

"I've had to face up to the fact that most of our society thinks of scientists as people who are likely to do something bad. Either bad to make money for themselves, or to cause trouble in the Frankensteinian sense." Douglas Melton, Harvard embryologist.

David Ewing Duncan, *The Geneticist Who Played Hoops with my DNA*, Frontispiece.

Most people agreed that it was wrong to control human reproduction in order to selectively enhance or delete certain features of the human race by purposely oppressing people with the undesirable traits. However, in the 1960s, Theodosius Dob-

# Caution is in Order

Many of those who speak, write, think, and vote about the future of genetics believe that once scientists master the science of cloning humans, animals and plants, and even extinct species, it is futile to try and prevent it. Instead, they advise that concerns are discussed openly, public input is gathered, and decisions are made thoughtfully. David Ewing Duncan interviewed seven prominent scientists to tell the story of stem cell research, cloning, and other genetic frontiers that are being crossed in the 21st century. In the prelude to his book *The Geneticist Who Played Hoops with my DNA,* Duncan sums up his impressions:

"Scientists need to be keenly aware of not only potential dangers, but the ethical and social impact of their discoveries. Yet I also believe that many of the discoveries and possibilities will happen regardless of what society thinks. As in splitting the atom, once the knowledge exists, the science will find a way to happen, possibly in secret in countries where neither ethics nor the public's fears much matter. This makes it even more crucial that this science be allowed to go forward while being closely watched, with appropriate safeguards."

David Ewing Duncan, *The Geneticist Who Played Hoops with my DNA,* pg. 15

zhansky, a Russian biologist first suggested that the ability to change people's genes might someday be possible. Furthermore, he believed that this gene manipulation was morally acceptable. Dobzhansky said there is a difference between selecting certain genes and selecting certain people.

Not everyone agrees that there is a distinction. But it turns out that Americans, at least, respond in different ways according to how the issue is presented. Lee Silver, the Princeton ethicist, explains in his book *Challenging Nature* that when Americans are asked about control of genetic inheritance, 86 percent believe that only God should have that power. However, when people are asked to consider certain genetic characteristics of their own child, the response is quite different. Given the choice, many people would change their children's genes to protect them from disease or make them smarter. Silver explains that this lack of consistency worries some ethicists and underscores their belief that society must absolutely guarantee that no one has the power to control the genetic destiny of others.

One thing is certain. People will never agree completely about cloning. As Gina Kolata explains: "Yet, if there is one lesson of cloning it is that there is no uniformly accepted way to think about the ethical questions that it [raises], and no agreement, even among the most thoughtful and well-informed commentators, about what is right and what is wrong."[51] This is a world filled with diverse, firmly held ideas and many interests. Perhaps the ultimate goal is not agreement, but the determination to listen well, consider all ideas carefully, trust that most people want to do what is right, and to strike a thoughtful balance.

**NOTES**

## Chapter One: Curing Disease

1. Gina Kolata, *Clone.* New York: William Morrow and Company, Inc. 1998, pg. 9.

2. Mike May, "Nature's Menders," *Understanding Cloning,* New York: Warner Books, 2002, pg. 72.

3. Dr. Michael W. Fox, *Beyond Evolution.* New York: The Lyons Press, 1999, pg. 109.

4. May, *Understanding Cloning,* pg. 75.

5. Quoted in Kenneth Chang, "Company Says It Used Cloning to Create New Kidneys for Cow," *New York Times,* January 31, 2002. http://query.nytimes.com/gst/fullpage.html?sec=health&res=9F0 7EFD71E3AF932A05752C0A9649C8B63.

6. Lee M. Silver, *Challenging Nature.* New York: HarperCollins, 2006, pg. 171.

7. The American Society for the Defense of Tradition, Family, and Property, "Ban All Human Cloning," April 23, 2002. http://www. tfp.org/TFPForum/TFPCommentary/ban_all_cloning.htm.

8. Alvin Powell, "From the Laboratory to the Patient," *Harvard University Gazette,* April 22, 2004. www.news.harvard.edu/ga-zette/2004/04.22/99-StemOver.html.

9. Deborah Blum, "A Pox on Stem Cell Research," *The New York Times,* August 1, 2006, pg. A19.

## Chapter Two: Improving Food

10. Andrew Pollack and Andrew Martin, "F.D.A. Tentatively Declares Food from Cloned Animals to Be Safe," *New York Times,* December 29. 2006, pg. A20.

11. Justin Gillis, "Clone Generated Milk, Meat May be Approved," *Washington Post,* October 6, 2005. http://www.washingtonpost. com/wp-dyn/content/article/2005/10/05/AR2005100502074. html.

12. Faye Flam, "Not Exactly Built to Code," *San Diego Union Tribune,* March 29, 2007, pg. E1.

13. Quoted in Gogoi, Pallavi. "Cloned Foods Pit Scientists Against Consumers," *Business Week* online, May 4, 2007. http://www.msnbc.msn.com/id/18434287/.

14. David Schubert, "Food From Cloned Animals," *San Diego Union Tribune,* January 3, 2007, pg. B7.

15. Fox, *Beyond Evolution,* pg. 112.

16. Henry I. Miller, "These Products Are Long Overdue," *San Diego Union Tribune,* January 3, 2007, pg. B7.

17. Barbara A. Mikulski, "People Have the Right to Know if They're Eating Cloned Food," *News from U.S. Senator Barbara A. Mikulski,* January 31, 2007. http://mikulski.senate.gov.

18. Daniel Charles, "Corn That Clones Itself Could Help Feed the Poor," *Wall Street Journal,* February 28, 2003. http://www.agnios.com/static/news/NEWSID_4087.php.

19. Daniel Charles, "Corn That Clones Itself Could Help Feed the Poor," *Wall Street Journal,* February 28, 2003. http://www.agnios.com/static/news/NEWSID_4087.php.

## Chapter Three: Saving the Animals

20. Robert Lana, Betsy Dresser, and Philip Damiani, "Cloning Noah's Ark," *Understanding Cloning,* pg. 23.

21. CBS News, "San Diego's Frozen Zoo," October 14, 2002. http://www.cbsnews.com/stories/2002/10/14/tech/main525521.shtml.

22. Gregory Pence, *Cloning After Dolly: Who's Still Afraid?* pg. 32.

23. Jacqui Hayes, "Back from the Dead," *Cosmos Online.* www.cosmosmagazine.com/node/903.

24. Jacqui Hayes, "Back from the Dead," *Cosmos Online.* www.cosmosmagazine.com/node/903.

25. Scott Weidensaul, "Raising the Dead," Audubon, May, 2002. http://magazine.audubon.org/features0205/raising_the_dead.html.

26. Scott Weidensaul, "Raising the Dead," Audubon, May, 2002. http://magazine.audubon.org/features0205/raising_the_dead.html.

27. Maryann Mott, "Cat Cloning Offered to Pet Owners," National

Geographic News, March 25, 2004. http://nationalgeographic. com/news/2004/03/0324_040324_catclones.html.

28. Scientific American.com, "But What About Rover and Fluffy?" November 17, 2000. http://www.sciam.com/article. cfm?articleID=000294FF-2290-1CBE-B4A8809EC588EEDF&m odsrc=related_links.

**Chapter Four: Making Babies**

29. Kolata, *Clone,* pg. 17.

30. Kolata, *Clone,* pg. 17.

31. Quoted in Courtney Campbell, "Cloning Human Beings," MS-NBC. http://www.msnbc.msn.com/id/3371684/.

32. David Ewing Duncan, *The Geneticist Who Played Hoops with My DNA.* New York: HarperCollins, 2005, pg. 53.

33. Leon R. Kass, M.D., "The Report of the President's Council on Bioethics", New York: Public Affairs, 2002, pg. 114.

34. Quoted in Kolata, *Clone,* pg. 102.

35. Kolata, *Clone,* pg. 105.

36. CNN.com "Raelian Leader Says Cloning First Step to Immortality," Feb. 12, 2004. http://archives.cnn.com/2002/HEALTH/12/27/human.cloning/index.html.

37. Gina Kolata, "A Cloning Scandal Rocks a Pillar of Science Publishing," *New York Times,* December 18, 2005. http://query.nytimes.com.

38. *Why Not Clone a Human?,* VHS. Princeton: Films for the Humanities and Sciences (ABC News), 1999.

**Chapter Five: The Future of Cloning**

39. *Why Not Clone a Human?*

40. Kolata, *Clone,* pg. 72.

41. Nigel M. de S. Cameron, M.L. Tina Stevens, "What California Can Learn from Korean Cloning Scandal," *SFGate.com.* http://sfgate.com/cgi-bin/article.cgi?file=/chronicle/archive/2005/12/13/EDG-I5G6BRN1.DTL.

42. Silver, *Challenging Nature,* pg. 135.

43. Jeff Zeleny, "House Votes to Expand Stem Cell Research," *New*

*York Times,* June 8, 2007, pg. A23.

44. Sheryl Gay Stolberg, "Bush Vetoes Bill Removing Stem Cell Limits, Saying 'All Human Life Is Sacred,' *New York Times,* June 21, 2007, pg. A21.

45. "The States Confront Stem Cells," *New York Times* editorial, March 31, 2006, pg. A20.

46. Terri Somers, "Worlds Apart," *San Diego Union Tribune,* December 17, 2006, pg. A22.

47. Arlene Judith Klotzko, *A Clone of Your Own?* Cambridge:Cambridge University Press, 2006, pg. 80.

48. ABCNews, "Therapeutic Cloning," Ask an Expert. http://www.abc.net.au/science/realexpert/cloning/Explore.

49. Nicholas Wade, "Biologists Make Skin Cells Work Like Stem Cells," *New York Times,* June 7, 2007, pg. 1.

50. Nicholas Wade, "Biologists Make Skin Cells Work Like Stem Cells," *New York Times,* June 7, 2007, pg. 1.

51. Kolata, *Clone,* pg. 16.

# DISCUSSION QUESTIONS

### Chapter One: Curing Disease

1. Why do scientists believe that it is important to clone embryos from people who suffer from diseases such as diabetes?

2. How do animal rights activists explain their opposition to the use of animals in cloning experiments?

3. How does 'therapeutic cloning' differ from 'reproductive cloning?'

### Chapter Two: Improving Food

1. Why are farmers concerned about public resistance to cloned foods—commonly called the 'yuck factor?'

2. Summarize the arguments both in favor of and opposed to the mandatory labeling of cloned foods.

3. According to the author, why do some people believe that seed companies have an interest in promoting the development of self-cloning corn?

### Chapter Three: Saving the Animals

1. Why do scientists want to use one species as surrogate mothers for another species? What obstacles stand in the way?

2. According to the author, why do some conservationists oppose the cloning of endangered species?

3. How would cloning the Tasmanian tiger affect the ecosystem of Australia?

4. Why do many people believe it is wrong to clone pets?

## Chapter Four: Making Babies

1. Explain the author's statement that lack of scientific knowledge will not be the major stumbling block to cloning?

2. Why would it be difficult to grow up as a clone?

3. Describe some of the ways in which clones and twins are alike and different.

## Chapter Five: The Future of Cloning

1. Explain the author's statement that human cloning will increase the gap between the rich and the poor.

2. Describe the advantages and disadvantages of using adult stem cells to treat disease.

3. What is the significance of the recent discovery that four genes may be responsible for changing skin cells into stem cells?

# ORGANIZATIONS TO CONTACT

**Americans to Ban Cloning**
1100 H St. NW
Suite 700
Washington, DC 20005
(202) 347-6840 • fax (202) 347-6849

The Americans to Ban Cloning (ABC) coalition is a group of concerned Americans and U.S. based organizations that promote a global, comprehensive ban on human cloning.

**Biotechnology Industry Organization (BIO)**
1201 Maryland Avenue, SW
Suite 900
Washington, DC 20024
(202) 962.9200

Biotechnology information, advocacy and network. This is the major organization of the biotechnology industry. Includes information about major developments in the field.

**The Humane Society of the United States**
2100 L Street, NW
Washington, DC 20037
(301) 258-8276 • fax: (301) 258-3078

This organization promotes the ethical treatment of animals. The website includes information on current issues and local humane societies throughout the United States.

**Organic Consumer's Association**
6771 South Silver Hill Drive
Finland MN 55603
(218) 226-4164 • fax (218) 353-7652

This watchdog association educates the public about health, genetic engineering, food safety, sustainable agriculture and other issues concerning organic farming and foods. Includes an archive of articles about cloning and patenting as well as recent cloning news.

**FOR MORE INFORMATION**

## Books

Holly Cefrey, *Cloning and Genetic Engineering* (High Interest Books), Danbury: Children's Press, 2002. Beautiful images help clarify cloning and genetic engineering. Explores social issues and future applications of cloning.

Sylvia Louise Engdahl, ed. *Cloning* (Contemporary Issue Companion). San Diego: Greenhaven Press, 2006. Explores the various medical, social, political and legal issues raised by cloning.

Nancy Harris, ed. *Exploring Science and Medical Discoveries—Cloning*. San Diego: Greenhaven Press, 2004. In-depth treatment of both natural and artificial cloning including current controversies and future applications.

Gary E. McCuen, *Cloning: Science & Society* (Ideas in Conflict Series). Hudson: GEM Publications, 1998. Each chapter presents readings from different perspectives about human and animal applications to cloning technology. Also present religious perspectives.

Sally Morgan, *Body Doubles: Cloning Plants and Animals* (Science at the Edge). Portsmouth: Heinemann Publications, 2002. Written for grades 5–8. Explores the issues raised by the ability of scientists to artificially clone plants and animals.

Sally Morgan, *From Sea Urchins to Dolly the Sheep: Discovering Cloning*. Portsmouth: Heinemann, 2006. Tells the story of cloning and its potential applications to farming and medicine.

Tamara Roleff, *Opposing Viewpoints Series—Cloning*. San Diego: Greenhaven Press, 2005. Presents various perspectives of issues raised by cloning.

## Web Sites:

**ActionBioscience.org.** (http://www.actionbioscience.org/bio-tech/pecorino.html). Lauren Pecorino, "Animal Cloning: Old MacDonald's Farm Is Not What it Used to Be" Good simple explanation of how animal cloning works and the issues involved in cloning animals.

**American Museum of Natural History.** (http://ology.amnh.org/genetics/cloning/index.html). All About Cloning. The American Museum of Natural History devotes this website to genetics and cloning. It includes a photograph of Ian Wilmut.

**How Stuff Works**. (http://www.howstuffworks.com/cloning.htm). Craig C. Freudenrich, Ph.D. "How Cloning Works. This comprehensive website explains how cloning works in both animals and plants. Includes many clear illustrations and a bibliography with links to related articles, news, and discussions about the ethics of cloning.

**Human Genome Project Information.** (http://www.ornl.gov/sci/techresources/Human_Genome/elsi/cloning.shtml). A very complete website that includes a "Cloning Fact Sheet" and many links to further information.

**Learn.Genetics.** (http://gslc.genetics.utah.edu/units/cloning/). A website for teachers and students. The link to "Click and Clone," is especially entertaining. Use the cursor to transfer a nucleus from a brown mouse into the egg of a black mouse, then grow the resulting embryo in a white mouse. Guess the color of the clone.

**PerPetuate.** (http://www.perpetuate.net/). This company, a subsidiary of Cyagra, a leader in animal cloning, promises to preserve the DNA from exceptional pets. Website describes the process of cloning a pet, lists prices of preserving pet DNA, and includes a gallery of pets whose DNA awaits cloning.

**The Reproductive Cloning Network**. (http://www.reproductivecloning.net/). A comprehensive site that supports reproductive and therapeutic human cloning. Includes articles, resources, and links to many other organizations that support human cloning.

**Science News for Kids.** (http://sciencenewsforkids.org/articles/20051019/Feature1.asp). Emily Sohn "From Stem Cell to Any Cell". A good overview of differences between embryonic and adult stem cells. Includes photographs of differentiated cells from various human organs. Clear description of stem cells: where they are found; an overview of the issues involved in using stem cells. Includes some good illustrations of actual human stem cells in various stages of development.

## DVD, Video, Radio

*Why Not Clone a Human?* (VHS) 1999.  Princeton: Films for the Humanities and Sciences (ABC News), 1999. Interviews with Princeton University's Lee Silver about cloning; Harvard's Stephen Jay Gould discusses Siamese twins. Discussions between Ted Koppel and Robert Krulwich, ABC News commentators.

"Reality Check," *This American Life,* National Public Radio, (http://www.sho.com/site/thisamericanlife/prevepisodes.do?episodeid=127169). Watch the first video episode of NPR radio show "This American Life" with Ira Glass, as he tells the story of the Reddells, who cloned their beloved pet Brahma bull named "Chance" and then had to contend with the unexpected nature of his genetic progeny, "Second Chance."

*The Future of Food,* Deborah Koons,  (DVD) Garcia Lily Films, 2004. (www.thefutureoffood.com). An in depth examination of the issues concerning the genetic engineering of foods. Many interviews with scientists and experts in the food and biotechnology industries.

# INDEX

# PICTURE CREDITS

# ABOUT THE AUTHOR

Tina Kafka is a teacher, who loves to learn. She lives in San Diego, California.